Illustrated

INDIAN
Motorcycle
BUYER'S ★ GUIDE™

Jerry Hatfield

Motorbooks International
Publishers & Wholesalers ®

This Second Edition published in 1995 by Motorbooks International Publishers & Wholesalers, PO Box 2, 729 Prospect Avenue, Osceola, WI 54020 USA

Motorbooks International books are also available at discounts in bulk quantity for industrial or sales-promotional use. For details write to Special Sales Manager at the Publisher's address

Library of Congress Cataloging-in-Publication Data available

ISBN 0-87938-999-0

On the front cover: 1941 Sport Scout owned by Dan Miller of Fremont, Ohio. Restoration by Indian Motorcycle Supply, Inc. *Hans Halberstadt*

Printed and bound in the United States of America

Contents

Acknowledgments

Thanks to all you friends and experts who made this book a reality. Without you, the book would still be nothing more than an idea.

Former Indian-staffer Bob Finn provided Indian archives negatives, which are the ultimate thrill for a collector like me. These produced outstanding photographs that appear throughout the book. Ex-staffers Matt Keevers and Jim Hill helped with research and copying of Indian-archives photographs. Matt and Peggy Keevers were my hosts during two visits to Indian's hometown, Springfield, Massachusetts. Former Indian-staffer Emmett Moore, also a co-founder of the Antique Motorcycle Club of America, provided rare photos. Champion Indian racer Ed Kretz, Sr., loaned his photo collection. Mary Kretz hosted several visits for interviews.

Stephen Wright, author of *American Racer*, loaned archives photographs. Ian Campbell expertly copied archives photographs. George Hays provided nearly forty photos from his large collection. Richard Renstrom, author of *Motorcycle Milestones*, gave photo support. Russ Cox, Richard Ostrowski and Sam Hotton provided photos. Don Doody made substantial editorial contributions.

Owners of restored Indians helped me catch their machines on film. These were: Marv Baker, Dick Barth, Dewey Bonkrud, Max Bubeck, Ed Carlson, John Eagles, Gene Grimes, Ray Hook, Richard Morris, Lee Standley and Chuck Vernon. Joseph Kulhavy and Paul Pearce responded to my telephone requests, and provided photos of their Indians. George Yarocki provided much information from his considerable literature collection. Earl Chalfant provided information.

Professional restorers Jeff Grigsby, Jake Junker, Bob Shingler and Bob Stark were invaluable sources of information.

Bob Shingler twice went to the trouble of photographing his collection of vertical twins and singles—the second time because I lost the first batch of negatives. Bob provided factory records on the verticals.

Bob Stark has been a friend for ten years, during which time he has patiently answered many a question about Indians. Much of my Indian enthusiasm comes from Bob. He carefully reviewed the manuscript and offered suggestions.

Preface

Indians were better than Harley-Davidsons, and if you don't believe that just ask any Indian fan.

"Why if only Indian had done things differently in 1916 . . ." somebody starts. Another Indian fan says, "No, 1948 was when they made their big mistake, and I'll tell you another thing. . . ." And so it goes.

The author at speed and at play.

Perhaps it's the might-have-beens that make the Indian motorcycle so alluring. If Harley-Davidson had gone under instead of Indian, I'm sure that Harleys would be my favorite motorcycles, but Indian bit the dust so Indian owns my soul.

I've owned and ridden motorcycles of every size and shape and purpose, but Indians are my solid favorite. Logical? I don't know. But in as much as the sport of motorcyling isn't the most logical of habits, I won't spend much time trying to explain what I don't even understand myself. I just know what I like, and that I like motorcycles, and that Indians give me the best combination of physical and mental kicks. "There's magic in the name Indian," the ads said. I agree.

Each Indian has a feel and a look that sets it apart from other steeds. They're all the better when you get to know their history, and you can imagine yourself as one or the other of the great Indian riders who battled with the dastardly Harley gang. Why just today, I was Cannonball Baker, setting another transcontinental record.

Jerry Hatfield
Garden Grove, California

Standards

There's a real problem here. A friend of mine asked me why I like my 1929 Scout 750 better than my 1947 Chief 1200. The Chief he reckoned as being faster and more comfortable than a Scout, a two-person bike instead of a solo, and easier to keep in spare parts than the older and smaller motorcycle. My friend was logical; I'm not. I told him I prefer

Total restorations aren't the only way to go, sample one. This circa 1915 41.57 ci Little Twin is totally original except for the front tire. The bike is probably worth more this way than restored. *George Hays*

the 1929 Scout to the 1947 Chief, because the Scout gives me more of what I like in an antique motorcycle. Besides coming in second on my friend's list of criteria, the Scout's noisier, cruder and obviously older—all qualities that are part of the illogical charm of old iron. An old motorcycle does things *for* you and *to* you, so you have to sort out how much of the attraction is physical and how much is mental.

An important factor to consider, although certainly not the deciding factor unless you make it so, is the cost of owning an Indian. In this book, I'll attempt to clarify the true cost of Indian motorcycles by presenting my opinions on the investment value of each model. Each Indian type is rated in terms of the likelihood of future value, with star ratings of one through five. A three-star motorcycle is one that will not cost you any-

thing to own over the long haul, because the motorcycle will appreciate enough to offset inflation. Likewise, a one-star is a financial loser, a two-star will cost you moderately, a four-star will make you a little money, and a five-star is better than money in the bank. These star ratings disregard normal operating expenses, so a motorcycle ridden 30,000 miles is going to cost you some money eventually, regardless of the machine's intrinsic appreciation.

Incidentally, I haven't rated sidecars on a blow-by-blow basis. Sidecars are rare, but demand is low. Generally, you should regard sidecars as three-star investments hitched to a whatever-star motorcycle. As for trikes, they're too rare to rate.

Buying and selling conditions will have much to do with how you make out over the long haul. I've always bought high and sold

Sample two. A good way to save money is to go for the period custom look. This is the author's bobber 1929 Model 101 Scout. Many Indians were fixed up this way, so the motorcycle is authentic, although not stock. The bike had just completed a 3,000 mile run when the photo was taken.

low, but you may be good at cutting deals. Allow a half-star variance for the deal; in other words, if you buy high and sell low you lose a full star, converting a three-star Indian into a two-star Indian. Be cunning on both ends, and your three-star Indian will work out as a four-star investment. Buy one way and sell another, and you'll have a three-and-a-half-star bike.

A rating system based on expected percentage value growth can lead to mind warp. Today's undesirable motorcycle—which can be bought cheaply—may fare well in the future when it may only be average undesirable. Conversely, by 1968, the 1941 Indian Fours had climbed to a price roughly equivalent to a then-new medium-priced Chevrolet. The 1941 Fours are still priced there today, and in the next century you should still be able to trade a good 1941 Four for a new middle-of-the-road Chevy. So in the value growth system, a 1941 Indian Four is a solid three-star motorcycle: you won't make anything on it, but the cost of ownership will be minimal. On the other hand, a 19XX junker can be a five-star investment value.

As the story goes, "Why, if only I had known how much these old things would appreciate, I would've bought one when they were new and left it in the original crate." But you would've lost a considerable sum by parking your money in that way. Any bank would give you a better return on your money, and you could now have several examples of the thirty-year-old warhorse. Things aren't that way for today's buyer of old iron, because we already know that Indian motorcycles are important historical pieces as well as fun critters, so everyone expects the value of Indian motorcycles to continue to rise. Still, remember that you aren't going to get rich with your Indian because these legendary motorcycles went through their bottoming out period long ago, when they were merely rusty, dusty and untrusty.

On a case-by-case basis, careful buying and selling can reward any owner of American-built Indians with zero or near-zero cost of ownership. The relative popularity of each Indian model makes it either easier or harder to sell than other Indians.

Models in high demand, such as late Chiefs, are less risky investments than low demand models, such as the 1933 Motoplane. Thus, although rarity can increase a model's value, rarity alone does not translate into a good investment. For a rare model to be a good investment, the model also has to be desirable. A motorcycle can be rare because nobody liked it when it was new. In such a case, don't be surprised if nobody likes it sixty years later. In summary, I've taken the risk factor into consideration, though not in any scientific way. Again, money isn't everything.

Many claim that the first and last years of a model command premium prices. I have no quarrel with that logic for serious collectors, although as a rider I couldn't care less about such psychology. It can also be difficult to determine the appropriate price premium for first- or last-year status. For example, the seller and buyer of an Indian Ace or Model 401 will seldom have any recent and reliable information about the market concensus on these motorcycles.

The importance of established market trends can be verified by studying the real estate industry, in which finance companies are reluctant to loan money for home sales in areas where comparable homes have not been sold in recent months. Anyway, the seller of an Indian Ace or Model 401 will strongly assert that these first-year models deserve a price premium, so the buyer will have to decide to what extent the asking price is traditional selling huff and puff, to what extent the seller sincerely believes in the premium and to what extent the seller's sincerity is matched by market knowledge. The scenario tends to be a contest of wills and patience—a risky situation for both seller and buyer.

I've been told that people are beginning to buy motorcycles primarily as investments, as they might buy stamps or a Van Gogh; hence, the investment value of a motorcycle is dominated by the speculative image of the machine as opposed to its physical attributes. Following this line of thought, collectible motorcycles will gradually become the property of people who are more affluent

Sample three. Another authentic non-stocker. This is Max Bubeck's 1949 vertical twin Scout with custom swinging-arm rear suspension. The rear frame structure was manufactured by the Martin company, mainly for Triumphs.

Bubeck had to build a jig to ensure proper installation. Thus configured, the bike won the 1962 Greenhorn Enduro and other events. As a piece of history, the motorcycle should be left this way, scratches, dents and all.

than motorcyclists as a whole, the property of the newly converted, so to speak.

I disagree because there's something about motorcycles that embarrasses the kind of people whose main concern is estate building. I think the main attraction of any kind of old motor vehicle is its hold on the imagination; an old vehicle either calls to mind youthful days or helps our imaginations put us in an era and environment we hold special. My view is, either you have the motorcycle bug or you don't. People who've been too conservative to be practicing motorcyclists, will not suddenly be trying to capture images they never cherished in the first place.

I also think that conservative people, non-motorcyclists in other words, are less likely to speculate on motorcycles than on more traditional collectibles. One doesn't want to have to apologize to one's friends for one's

collection, does one? Except for the F-heads, the bulk of price pressure will continue to come from those who view the motorcycle with passion—the true believers, the motorcycle people. This means that inflation-adjusted prices of Indian motorcycles, unlike Bugatti automobiles, are constrained from rising indefinitely. If I'm right, twenty years from now people will still be able to make a living maintaining and restoring Indians because motorcyclists will still be riding them. On the other hand, if motorcycles are just alternatives to oil paintings, the well will run dry because Indian motorcycles will become static displays.

Let's talk about prices. I'll give you some idea of prices by comparing Indian price ranges with the suggested retail price of a popular Harley-Davidson model. I think this will keep the text from being overcome by inflation. I've chosen the FLHTC Electra

Glide as the reference Harley because it appears to be a model that will be in the Harley-Davidson range for a long time. As of January, 1995 the suggested retail price of the FLHTC Electra Glide was $14,000 (with AM/FM radio and tape deck) but dealers were actually charging over $16,000 for this model.

The actual dealer's price is the cost comparison basis to be used throughout the book. The FLHTC is equipped with 80ci V-twin engine, five-speed gearbox, handlebar fairing, front and rear crash guards, saddlebags, and fender-top luggage box.

My estimated Indian price ranges include the original purchase price plus all cosmetic and technical work and materials required to complete restoration. The next statement is critical to your understanding: in estimating restoration costs I assume that you will hire out all work and that the end product will be in near-concours condition. This assumption tends to level out the wide ranges of prices being asked by sellers, since in a few words an advertiser can't—or doesn't want to—make clear just how well-restored the motorcycle is. Asking prices are all over the map, and so are conditions of restoration. The point where they meet is the point of sale when the motorcycle can be seen by the potential buyer. A range of twenty percent is typically quoted because that accounts for the luck factor. For example, a friend of mine bought a concours-restored 1949 Indian vertical twin for $3,000, decided he didn't like it, and sold it ten days later for $4,000!

Don't let the estimated prices scare you. The fully and professionally restored prices, while providing a more consistent basis of comparison, are on the high end of the scale. You don't have to have your Indian restored to near-concours status to have lots of fun. My 1947 was a grade below the near-concours status, and I had loads of fun with it for nine years. My 1929 Scout is a non-stock custom with abbreviated fenders, and it draws just as much attention from the public as if it were a show-winner. The Scout is also just as much fun to ride as if it were a near-concours. Anyway, you don't have to tie up the family fortune in an Indian by going the whole restoration route. You can stick your toes in the water for half the price, and have fun while you are waiting for more money or deciding whether you want to go the whole route.

Sample Four. Another way to save money is to restore in moderation. The cockpit of the author's 1947 shows several money-saving decisions. The headlight is an aftermarket replacement then priced at $84; the exact reproduction item with slightly different shape and different lettering then cost $125. Windshield and handlebar clamps are cadmium-plated like the originals, whereas most Chiefs are restored with more expensive chrome plating. The ammeter is a nice imitation, and only an expert such as a motorcycleshow judge can tell the difference from the more costly real thing. Low-level handlebars are genuine 1947 items, but most riders spend over $100 extra for replica high bars. This gearshift lever is painted silver instead of chromed, and unrepaired pitting isn't that obvious. Gas and oil caps are used items. Tanks are from a 1948 Chief, and the small 1948 style cutout notch behind the panel hasn't been filled in. The used Harley seat was bought for $40, whereas a deluxe leather buddy seat costs over $300. Other cost-savers, not shown, include used exhaust system, as-is fender trim, unmatched engine and frame numbers, and minor bodywork irregularities. Despite these cost-saving imperfections, this motorcycle always made a favorable impression and looked good enough to be pictured in a magazine. Total savings of cost-cutting approach exceeded $1,000 in 1978, and would save about $3,000 in 1995. It's up to you; the object is to have fun.

I'll tell you about the history of each Indian, because that's part of the fun of the Indian cult and because each model's history affects its value. I'll describe what it's like to ride several of the more well-known models. There's still room for usability as a criterion, meaning the time-honored factors by which new motorcycles have always been judged: speed, acceleration, handling, comfort, reliability, maintainability and economy. But even here, one is struck by the fact that motorcycle A can score higher in each of these areas than motorcycle B, yet B can be more fun than A.

Since rating Indian motorcycles is a personal thing, I'm going to give you my personal vote as well as the market value. In the formula, I'll include the opinions of experts, long-time Indian riders who did most of their riding when Indians were still rolling through the factory doors, men who know Indians inside and out from years of wrench turning. You may be surprised to learn that the experts' experiences are varied, and their motivations and voices diverse. Motorcycling has always been this way, each rider convinced his steed is obviously superior to his buddy's. Why should life be different among Indian motorcycle enthusiasts?

My job in writing this book isn't to make you agree with me. Instead, I'm here to arm you with the facts that will help you decide for yourself just how and if you want to live the Indian motorcycle experience. We'll have fun together in these pages, and you'll have the time of your life when you venture down your chosen Indian trail.

★★★★	1901-1915 F-head, singles and twins
★★★	1916-1925 Powerplus singles and twins
Not ratable	1916 Model K Featherweight
Not ratable	1917-1918 Model O Light Twin
★★	1925-1928 Prince, side-valves and overhead-valves
Not ratable	1908-1931 racers and hillclimbers

Early models 1901-1931

History
1901-1908

A fondness for history has something to do with one's urge to collect Indian motorcycles, and the history of each model has something to do with its market value. Serious students of Indian history should read Harry V. Sucher's *The Iron Redskin*, which treats every aspect of the complex Indian story. The task here is a simpler one: to give you a collector's sense of history for each Indian model. So, we go down our own trail of Indian history.

George Hendee, a former high-wheel bicycle racing champion, was already manufacturing bicycles when he met Oscar Hedstrom at a bicycle race in 1900. Hedstrom was demonstrating a superior motor-powered pacing bicycle of his own design and manufacture; like many early motorcycles, the machine was used to provide a slipstream for pedalers who were trying for speed or endurance records. Hendee and Hedstrom decided to team up and manufacture what they called the Indian *motocycle* in Springfield, Massachusetts.

The engine design featured inlet-over-exhaust valve gear, then the standard of the young automotive field. Across the Atlantic, the motor press generally refers to these engines as inlet-over-exhaust (IOE), but I'll use the American term F-head. A concern in these early days of metallurgy was exhaust valve failure. In F-head motors, the idea was that the exhaust valve could be kept from getting too hot by placing the relatively cool inlet valve just above it. Also in line with standard practice, the inlet valve was actuated by cylinder vacuum, with only a small valve spring to assist in valve closing.

The flywheels were of open or webbed construction, the outer rim of each flywheel encircling a beam that was drilled for crank-

A 1906 model with optional acetylene lighting, which was first offered in 1905. Principal changes from the 1901 models are the cartridge spring front fork and left-hand twistgrip throttle introduced in 1905. Oil is carried in a separate compartment in the forward portion of the "camel-back" tank over the rear fender. Indian called this frame layout the diamond frame. The large tube above the front downtube contains the dry-cell batteries. The small conical-capped tube contains the ignition coil. *Indian archives/ Bob Finn*

Year and model	1906 Indian
Engine	F-head single
Bore and stroke	2⅝x3¼ in.
Displacement	17.59 ci
Bhp	2¼
Lubrication	total loss
Ignition	three dry-cell batteries, good for 800-2,000 miles
Gearbox	single-speed, final drive by chain
Clutch	none
Primary drive	single-row chain
Wheelbase	48 in.
Wheels and tires	23 in. wheels, 23x2.25 tires
Suspension	front, cartridge double cushion fork; rear, rigid
Weight	115 lb. (serviced)
Seat height	36 in.
Mpg	75
Oil consumption	200-400 miles/qt., depending on speed
Top speed	30 mph

shaft and mainshaft installation. In other words, the flywheels resembled wheels with two fat spokes.

Lubrication was through a total-loss system. Oil was pumped to the engine but not returned to the oil tank, all oil being consumed by the motor. For extra-hard pulling, in deep sand, up long hills and so on, the rider had an auxiliary hand pump. To set up one of these total-loss motors was a trial-and-error process, and moreover, the oil pump adjustment had to be tailored to the riding habits of the owner. Too much oil pumping meant fouled plugs; too little meant disaster.

The electrical system was also total loss; in other words, there was no generator. Instead, dry-cell batteries provided enough power for 800 to 2,000 miles of riding.

At first glance, a 1901 Indian looked like an ordinary pedal bicycle with a motor attached as an afterthought. The front fork was rigid, the power was transmitted from the engine shaft by a short chain to the underslung drive sprocket, and the control system featured two small hand levers. At the forward end of the top frame tube, the 1901-1903 Indians had a lever for controlling the carburetor. On the right side of the steering head was a lever that controlled the ignition timing and lifted the exhaust valve.

All Indians were finished in dark blue enamel. Changes were minimal through the end of the 1903 season.

In 1904, optional finishes included black and the famous Indian Red, then simply called vermillion. This was a dark hue which

Circa 1908 model, showing optional gear-driven primary drive. The oil tank is now located behind the cylinder. The rectangular box on the front downtube is for the dry-cell batteries and tools. Coarse-cut primary-drive gears were noisy. *George Hays*

Year and model	1908 Indian twin-cylinder
Engine	F-head 42 degree V-twin
Bore and stroke	2¾x3¼ in.
Displacement	38.61 ci
Bhp	5
Valve actuation	mechanical exhaust valve, mechanical or optional automatic (suction) inlet valve
Lubrication	total loss
Ignition	Standard: Indian special dry-cell batteries, good for 800-2,000 miles. Optional: three regular No. 6 dry-cells, or magneto
Gearbox	single-speed, final drive by chain
Clutch	none
Primary drive	gear
Wheelbase	51 in.
Wheels and tires	23 in. wheels, 23x2.25 tires
Suspension	front, cartridge double cushion fork; rear, rigid
Weight	135 lb. (serviced)
Seat height	36 in.
Mpg	60-80
Oil consumption	200-400 miles/qt., depending on speed
Top speed	60 mph (with racetrack gearing)

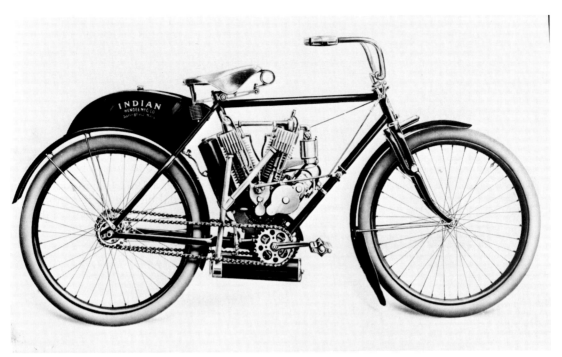

A 1908 twin. All 1901 through 1908 Indians featured the diamond frame, which was last offered in 1909 as a lower-cost option to the new loop frame. *Indian archives/Bob Finn*

Indian's first production racer was this 1908 model. Restoration by Stephen Wright.

some collectors call Hiram Walker red, after the whiskey bottle label. The original Indian Red was destined to remain in use until the 1940s, when it was supplanted by a brighter hue.

Twistgrip spark control was featured. Indian bragged throughout its existence that it was the first with the twistgrip control, but the 1904 Curtiss also had such a control.

The Indian system consisted of rods, bell-cranks and universal joints, a unique concept that was supposed to be troublefree but proved otherwise. When the handlebars were turned to extreme right or left the sliding joints would sometimes fall out, or bind so that an attempt to return the handlebars towards the center would result in bending the telescoping tubes.

The steering-head-mounted lever was retained, but now served to control the throttle. Incidentally, on these earliest Indians the primary speed control was considered to be the ignition timing, so the control setup had Indian riders using their right hand to vary speed, an ironic point because Indian was noted for left-hand speed control (by throttle) throughout most of the Redskin's history.

The power rating was 2¼ hp. The color was dark royal Indian Blue. Tires were 1¾ in. pneumatics.

The cushion fork was introduced in 1905, and consisted of pivoted lower fork blades acting on a horizontally mounted spring. While this was an improvement over the former unsprung front fork, the softened ride was gained at the expense of back-and-forth wheel movement that became objectionable at higher speeds. In the same year, Indian introduced the left-hand twistgrip throttle.

Detail changes to the motorcycle were made from 1905 through 1907, including a variety of saddles tailored to the weight of the rider, and additional color options. Power grew to 2¾ hp, tires to 2 in. and weight to 115 lb., while several kinds of commercial and pleasure three-wheelers were offered.

The biggest news for 1907 were Indian's

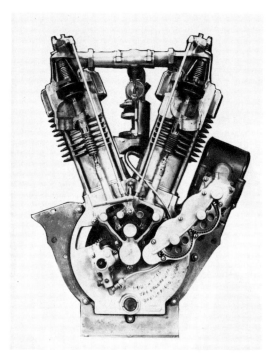

Cutaway display of F-head engine. The single camshaft is revealed. Hedstrom carburetor featured concentric float and rotating slotted drum instead of butterfly valve. *Indian archives/Bob Finn*

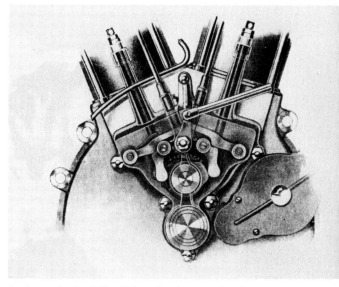

A closer look at the F-head valve mechanism. Crankshaft driving gear and camshaft-driven gear were inside the crankcase instead of the outer timing chest. *Indian 1915 catalog*

first cataloged V-twins, these being offered as 39 ci road models or 60 ci racers.

Substantial changes occurred in 1908, including the optional gear-driven primary drive, mechanical or automatic intake valves, and the new magneto ignition. Single-cylinder engines were offered in 19, 27 and 30 ci versions.

Models with mechanical inlet valves, whether twins or singles, used one inlet cam and one exhaust cam. The twins achieved this economy of motion through bellcrank lifters which enabled each cam to service

Riding a 1908 single

An early Indian single looks just like what it is, a motorbike, or as we call it today, a moped. As a motorcyclist, your expectations are low. You remind yourself that the whole purpose of motorcycles was still evolving back in 1908. People didn't even know what to call these things. The term autocycle floated around for a while, along with motor bicycle, and Indian settled on their own name, motocycle.

Motorcycles weren't primarily sports vehicles then, although sport was catching up with utility as the main drawing card. Moreover, there weren't any established ideas about how powered two-wheelers should look, so the design was purely practical. An early Indian looks the way it does because it happens to work well the way it's built. If there was any underlying styling strategy, that strategy was to present the motorcycle as something that looked not that different from and therefore not that much more difficult and dangerous to operate than a pedal bike. On that score, Indian management was pretty smart, just like today's moped builders. Or did the motorbike-look happen simply because the factory hadn't given any thought to making their motorcycles look distinctive? We'll never know.

Back to the ride.

After a few moments of reflection, your mind is in the right gear, and you're ready to measure the 1908 Indian single by the proper standards. Astride the bike, you lean it left and right to get the feel. This is a pleasant chore because there's only some 120 lb. to throw about.

You're instructed by the bike's owner on the starting drill, which consists of releasing the cylinder compression by lifting the exhaust valve pedaling off on the Indian and dropping the exhaust valve. The owner completes the briefing with the statement that you'll catch on to the left-hand throttle quickly. You wonder about that. The owner orders you to move your right hand away from the spark control grip so you won't feel like twisting it, and says that this will keep you atuned to the whereabouts of the all-important left-hand throttle.

You pedal away and get as much speed as you can while staying on the seat. In a few moments you twist the right grip inward as you would do to add throttle on other motorcycles. On the Indian, this action instead drops the exhaust valve, and the Indian fires up and starts gaining speed. Cautiously, and awkwardly, you twist the left grip inward to add power. Now the Indian is purring quietly along at about 15 mph, and you settle into the rhythm of the steady beat.

Riding this bike is purely a mental trip, for the thrill comes from appreciating the historical significance of the machine and just how well the Indian was built in 1908. The front wheel bounces back and forth under the action of the cushion fork, like a Schwinn bicycle of the 1950s. The fork chatters in a subdued way, the seat springs squeak, the breeze whistles in your ears and underneath all of this you hear the little motor puffing as though it'll run forever. You twist the throttle for more speed, and the Indian gathers momentum until you reach what you figure is about 30 mph. Now the bike has lost the effortless feel, and while you believe all is well down below, you back off again and get back to the little single's specialty, the 15 to 20 mph gait.

Built for a public accustomed to the bicycle and unfamiliar with the mysteries of the internal combustion engine, the early Indians were right on target. These motocycles were friendly in appearance, and the precision of construction was obvious. A brand-new one, even today, would be practical for neighborhood jaunts. You puff back to the starting line with increased respect for designer Oscar Hedstrom.

A 1909 loop-frame twin, first year of this design.
Original machines still featured block-lettered
Indian label. Restoration by Dewey Bonkrud.

A 1910 two-speed restored by the late J. Worth
Alexander. This was the first year of the leaf
spring fork. Most 1910 models featured block-lettered Indian name, but some had Indian
script as shown here. The abbreviated front
fender is authentic. *George Hays*

both cylinders. In profile, lifters looked something like a thumb and index finger squeezing on the opposite sides of the cam. The idea of using a minimum of valve lifting parts became a hallmark of Indian design, and continued on all V-twins for the rest of Indian's history.

Still another departure from the previous year was the first racing machine built for public sale. Since the birth of Indian, the marque had dominated racing, record setting and reliability trials, and the company realized the importance of maintaining a strong racing position.

1909-1913

Up to this point, Indian design clearly showed its bicycle roots in the frame construction, which the company called the diamond frame. Other manufacturers such as Harley-Davidson were evolving their frame design independent of the bicycle concept, with the frame forming a loop around the engine. Indian brought out their first loop frame as an optional feature in 1909, thus establishing the historical benchmark that would end forever the thought that the Indian might stay a sort of motor-bicycle.

Closeup of accessory passenger seat. Goodies like these enhance the value of an antique motorcycle. *George Hays*

A 1911 belt-drive Indian, built to satisfy a minority market. Block lettering was still used on some models, but Indian script was on most. Restoration by Lysle Parker. *George Hays*

The loop frame gave a lower center of gravity than the diamond frame; moreover, the loop frame was more visually appealing. The changeover was a rare moment in Indian history, as Indian usually set styling trends instead of following them. Both diamond- and loop-framed models were available throughout the year; the company was using up its supply of diamond frames and components, and a price break was given to those who purchased the old-style diamond-framed machines.

In 1909, there were numerous optional items, including a choice of tires, footrests, seats, longer handlebars and torpedo-shaped tanks for the diamond-framed models. The optional gray finish was no longer available.

Indian had been dedicated to chain drive, but when some dealers reported sales lost to competing belt-drive marques, the company responded with a conventional belt-drive single. The 1909 layout was a one-year-only configuration.

There were four big changes for 1910. The first was the replacement of the car-tridge fork with the leaf spring fork that was to be an Indian feature until 1946. The new fork brought with it an abbreviated front fender which stopped short of the steering head, the leaf spring evidently considered sufficient deterrent to road spray.

The second and third changes were the free engine and two-speed gearbox, although only a few Indians were equipped with these features. Prior to the free engine—an engine with a clutch between it and the gearbox— riders were obliged to kill their engines when coming to a halt, and then to restart by pushing or pedaling. The last big change was the availability of footboards on some models.

Indian included a new sophisticated belt-drive single in the 1910 range. This machine had a large engine pulley with internal sun or planetary gears; the pulley helped minimize belt slippage by providing a wide con-

Circa 1911 big-base eight-valve racer. Only two or three are believed to exist. All eight-valve twins had a small and a large exhaust valve teamed in each cylinder, the smaller valve opening slightly before the larger. Four-valve singles also used this setup. *D. O. Kinnie collection/ Russ Cox*

Circa 1914 small-base eight-valve racer. The sight glass at the bottom of the crankcase gave a quick check on oil level prior to starting. This feature was included on road models through the Powerplus generation. Restoration by Stephen Wright. *Sam Hotton*

tact arc. Indian found the expense of providing the system unwarranted by sales, however, and discontinued this design at year-end.

In 1911, the free engine was sold in considerable number as an extra-cost option for the 4 hp single and 7 hp twin. With an eye still on the belt-drive market, a conventional belt-drive motorcycle was offered. The total number of two-wheelers cataloged had grown to eight, including choices of battery or magneto ignition, two sizes of singles and twins, and optional chain or belt drive. The belt-drive single was fitted with a conventional handlever control for the idler pulley.

The company reaped a harvest of good publicity when its team took the first three places in the internationally contested Tourist Trophy race on the Isle of Man, off the west coast of England. This is the only TT win ever scored by an American-made motorcycle. By year-end, Indian held every American speed and distance record.

Capitalizing on the Tourist Trophy win, Indian introduced their 1912 Tourist Trophy singles and twins, which featured a separate foot starter mounted forward of the engine and actuated by a forward kick. Previously, starting had been by the bicycle-type pedals common on motorcycles of the day. Footboards were now the norm instead of the exception. Another advance was the double rear brake, featuring an external contracting band actuated by foot pedal and an internal expanding shoe actuated by hand lever. This evidently was partly motivated by the British requirement to provide each motorcycle with two brakes; Indian had a healthy business in Britain.

The model line-up for 1912 was reduced from eight to six by the elimination of the battery ignition option. The free engine, previously offered on only two models, was now obtainable on all Indians. A two-speed transmission was also available. A few belt-drive singles were sold to eliminate stocks of this relatively unpopular Indian, and there would be no more belt-drive redskins.

Reacting to public acceptance, Indian Red was now the standard finish.

Richard Morris pedaling off his 1913 single-speed twin. The other way of starting was to pedal down the road bicycle-style and then drop the exhaust valve.

Closeup of the Indian cradle spring frame introduced in 1913. Restoration by Dewey Bonkrud. *Sam Hotton*

Riding a 1913 twin

Before going through the starting ritual, you have a trial sitting and are immediately surprised at the tall-in-the-saddle stance. Designers hadn't yet gotten around to worrying about lowering the saddle height, a point that would become a doctrine in the mid-1920s. Sitting way up there in the 1913 ozone, you understand why public reaction would eventually demand something be done about the high perch. True, the rear stand is down right now, and that adds a couple of inches to the altitude, but you allow for this and conclude you'll get a tractor-high ride in a few minutes.

And how about these handlebars! They're so long they remind you of a wheelbarrow. You can almost reach out from the handgrips with your thumbs and touch your waist. In 1913, they rode below 30 mph most of the time.

The owner lets you do the work while he or she takes care of the engineering. While you're holding the handlebars down close to the steering head, the owner straddles the front wheel and manipulates both twistgrips. You rise from the saddle and begin pedaling.

This 1913 twin is a far cry from the early singles. A few years before, the moped concept and general smallness of the early Indian singles gave starting a genteel character. But pedaling this 61 ci twin is hard work.

As you begin to huff and puff, you remind yourself that you shouldn't be surprised if several minutes are required to fire up the twin. After all, these old-timers are typically ridden only five or six times a year, and unless the starting combination has been written down there may be a memory problem. Another point you've picked up from the enthusiasts is that carburetor wear wreaks havoc with starting and low-speed idling, and as this owner may not have gone to the trouble and expense of completely refurbishing the mixing pot, he or she may get to help you kick after you tire out. Prolonged pedaling would've been intolerable to the original owner back in 1913, but on the show scene a little extra exertion seems to be part of the fun. You wish you didn't have time to think about all this.

After what seems an eternity, the old bike starts, just about the time you're ready to take a rest. Actually, only twenty seconds or so have gone by, but it seems longer. There's a lot of smoke out back, but the owner says it'll get better after the motorcycle is warmed up. Journalists back in 1913 sometimes referred to motorcycles as *chuff* bikes, and now you know why. The noise isn't like the motorcycle's roar you've come to know. The noise is most akin to the sound of a one-cylinder lawn mower as there are two cylinders firing at the uneven pace that is the hallmark of all V-twins—sort of a cha-chuff, cha-chuff. There's also a lot of valve gear noise. Didn't you hear something like this at that antique farm equipment show a few months ago?

Next you push the Indian forward so that it comes off the rear stand, and then you hold the bars while your instructor lifts up the stand and stores it behind the spring clip on the rear fender. The owner takes control again and plays games with the right-hand ignition control, the left-hand throttle and the choke. After about three minutes of this ritual, he has the old iron horse idling at an unbelievably slow pace—cha-chuff, cha-chuff, cha-chuff—and you think that at any moment the dark red beast will sigh deeply, or perhaps belch, then fall into silence. The owner remarks that something really should be done about that worn-out carburetor so this bike will idle slower! Ah yes, you tell yourself, those were the days when motorcycles had big flywheels, and motors could spin steadily at a couple of hundred rpm.

All the cha-chuffing has things moving up and down, back and forth. You feel as though you're sitting on a bicycle with a Harley-Davidson Sportster engine idling just above the pedals. In a way, that's the deal, because you're straddling 61 ci, 1000 cc of locomotion. Newer bikes are faster, but you've never gotten such a kick from a motorcycle while idling in neutral. You wonder if you could lose weight after a few hours of this.

Indian had an optional two-speed gearbox in 1913, but this bike is a single-speeder so you'll have to be careful to keep from stalling while getting away. You set the left-hand throttle at about one-fourth turn, so the motor sounds as if it's doing 40 mph, then move your left hand to the long lever on the left side of the tank and ease the lever backward. You can't help wondering why the clutch lever wasn't on the right side for easier operation with the left-hand throttle. With a little right foot paddling, you're rolling and then "up" to 6 or 8 mph, then definitely airborne with both feet up on the floorboards where they belong. Hey, the floorboards are way down there, and your legs are only slightly bent at the knees! Stop trying to twist the right grip; it only slows things down.

Now that you're rolling along at about 25 mph, you realize that the one-speed transmission isn't as big a handicap as you expected. You nurse the right-hand grip clockwise, thus causing the spark to occur later on each power stroke, until at last the grip is at the limit. The monster flywheels do the rest, and there you are, smoothly cha-chuffing at something less than ten miles an hour. Until some brainy science fiction lover, inspired by countless stories, builds a real time machine, a Hedstrom-designed Indian must be the closest thing to it. Cannonball Baker set many a record on Indians similar to this.

No need to study brakes and acceleration and comfort, for these are not the measures of the Indian experience offered by founders Hendee and Hedstrom. All too soon, you're moving the long clutch hand lever to slip the clutch, then retarding the ignition by twisting the right grip, then cha-chuffing slowly back into present time.

Getting a forty-year jump on the rest of the world, Indian introduced swinging arm rear suspension in 1913, dubbing their creation the cradle spring frame. The rigid frame was continued as an option. Footboards were now provided on all models, not just the TT editions, and luggage racks were standard fare on all Indians. The ever-growing popularity of Indian Red spelled the demise of the original dark Indian Blue, which was no longer listed as an optional finish.

The V-twin was in full flower now, so eminently suited for America's long distances and rough roads which required large motorcycles for serious touring. Ninety percent of the 1913 Indian production was devoted to twin-cylinder machines.

A 1913 twin fitted with the 1915 and later three-speed transmission. Restoration by Dewey Bonkrud.

Three-speed transmission introduced in 1915. Parts of these gearboxes were still usable on the last 1953 Indians! *Indian 1916 catalog*

Racing support continued as a keystone of Indian management strategy. Although Indian didn't win the Isle of Man TT again, the firm continued to support this event and Indians placed consistently high. Stateside, Indian motorcycles ruled in dirt-track races, road races, hillclimbs and the spectacular board-track races conducted on quarter-mile or shorter ovals. The latter featured banked turns with slopes as steep as sixty degrees! For factory riders, Oscar Hedstrom designed four-valve singles and eight-valve twins, with all valves overhead.

1914-1915

In 1914, Indian created a sensation with the Hendee Special which featured electric

The saddle height of 31 in. is demonstrated by Bonkrud. Vertical distance from seat to middle of floorboards is 22.5 in., about four inches more than most modern bikes.

starting and electric lights. Unfortunately, batteries in 1914 were unreliable and the Hendee Special earned a bad reputation which limited its career to this year only. Four or five original Hendee Specials are known to exist. One or more imitations have been constructed over the years.

The three-speed countershaft transmission was launched in 1915. In principle, this transmission layout was destined to remain in production throughout Indian history; some 1915 transmission parts are usable in 1953 transmissions.

In the Indian three-speed transmission, the shift linkage moved a pair of gears back and forth along a shaft running the length of the gearbox. This sliding "double" gear was meshed with the "triple" gears mounted on a parallel shaft below the sliding double gear shaft. For shifting into low and second, the rider had to use the shift lever to mesh gears into gears. In contrast, in a modern constant-mesh transmission the rider causes dogs and slots to engage in the center of gears while the power-transmitting teeth along the gears' circumferences stay constantly in mesh. In the Indian three-speed, dog en-

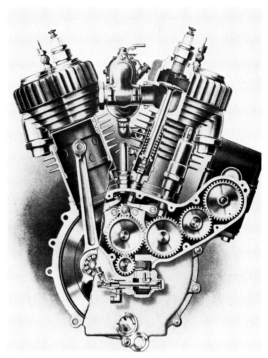

Powerplus engine continued the F-head-style single-camshaft layout. Heads and barrels were one piece. *Indian 1916 catalog*

The 1916 Powerplus had the F-head-style fuel tank and controls. A first-year Powerplus is more sought-after than later Powerpluses be-cause of status and appearance. Optional electric lights were first offered in 1914. Restoration by the late J. Worth Alexander. *George Hays*

J. Worth Alexander and his 1916 Powerplus single. All single and twin parts were shared with the exception of the crankcase. Powerplus singles are less common than twins, yet twins bring higher prices. Period leather cap and bow-tie were a nice touch. *George Hays*

Priming the cylinders with a syringe. Obviously a posed deal, this procedure was only required in very cold weather. The little syringe was removed from the tank top. Gasoline was squirted into the priming cup, a tapered valve which had been opened by turning the cup head counter-clockwise. After priming, the priming cups were closed. *George Hays*

gagement was used only for high gear.

Joining the 61 ci, 1000 cc twin was the Little Twin, at 42 ci. An improved kickstarter was adopted.

The 1915 Indians were the last of the line of machines designed by Hedstrom and managed by Hendee, both of whom had become disenchanted with the financiers who held controlling interest in the Indian company. Hedstrom had already left as a wealthy man, opting for early retirement on his Connecticut estate. During the year, Hendee, too, spent much of his huge earnings on a country home, and retired to watch his cattle graze.

The next generation of Indian motorcycles would be better machines, yet would not have the same character as the F-heads. Coincidentally, many years later the Horseless Carriage Club of America (HCCA) would pick as its dividing line the year 1915. As a result, the founders' Indians are eligible for HCCA events, while later Redskins are excluded from these status affairs. This factor raises the prices and expected value growth of the Hendee and Hedstrom horses.

1916-1918

The big news was the radically different Powerplus engine with side-by-side valves.

A 1916 Powerplus in merry flight. White tires were the rule through circa 1924, when black tires were phased in. *George Hays*

A 1916 Model K Featherweight three-speed. A failure, the model was available only one year. Catalog shots showed bicycle pedals for foot-rests instead of small floorboards and car-style clutch pedal instead of rocker clutch pedal. Restoration by Paul Pearce. *Paul Pearce*

The side-valve concept had been catching on across the Atlantic for five years, but had been seen in the United States only in the relatively unpopular Reading Standard motorcycle. The new 1916 side-valve machines were the brain child of Charles Gustafson, Sr., who earlier had supervised Reading Standard development.

The new layout met with sales resistance by confirmed Indian fans loyal to Hedstrom's F-heads, but a Powerplus test ride was sufficient to convert them because of the extra punch of the new side-valve engine. Indian

```
Year and model . . . . . . . . . . . . . . . . . . 1916 Featherweight
Engine . . . . . . . . two-stroke single with outside flywheel
Bore and stroke . . . . . . . . . . . . . . . . . . . . . . . . 2½x2¾ in.
Displacement . . . . . . . . . . . . . . . . . . . . 13½ ci, 221.2 cc
Bhp . . . . . . . . . . . . . . . . . . . . . . . . . . . . . . . . . . . . . . . . . 2½
Lubrication . . . . . . . . . . . . . . . . . . . . . . . . . . . . . oil mist
Ignition . . . . . . . . . . . . . . . . . . . . . . . . . . . . . . . . magneto
Gearbox . . . three-speed, hand-actuated, sliding-gear type
Clutch . . . . . . . . . . . . . . . . . . . . . . . . . . . . . . . . . . . . . . dry
Primary drive . . . . . . . . . . . . . . . . . . . . . single-row chain
Wheelbase . . . . . . . . . . . . . . . . . . . . . . . . . . . . . 46¾ in.
Wheels and tires . . . . . . . . . . . 21 in. wheels, 21x2.25 tires
   (catalog reference is 26x2.25 measured across tire dia.)
Suspension . . . . . . . . front, coil spring cushion cartridge;
   rear, rigid
Weight . . . . . . . . . . . . . . . . . . . . . . . . . . 225 lb. (est.)
Seat height . . . . . . . . . . . . . . . . . . . . . . . . . . . . 29 in.
Mpg . . . . . . . . . . . . . . . . . . . . . . . . . . . . . . . . . . . . . . 100
Oil consumption . . . . . . . . . . . . . . . . . . . . 50 miles/qt.
Top speed . . . . . . . . . . . . . . . . . . . . . . . 35 mph (est.)
```

Lysle Parker pilots his 1917 Powerplus sidecar outfit. New for 1917 were the streamlined tank and the two gold pinstripes with black center. This was last year of the rod-and-bellcrank controls. *George Hays*

A 1917 Model O Light Twin. At a price of $180, the Light Twin was too expensive to compete with used cars. Restoration by Paul Pearce. *Paul Pearce*

claimed the new motor developed more horsepower per cubic inch than any other motorcycle engine. From the international perspective the claim was merely advertis-

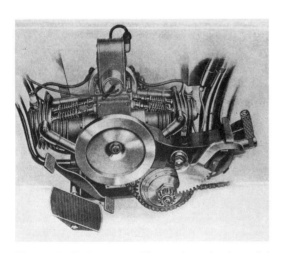

The Light Twin motor. The rocker clutch pedal stayed at any position the rider placed it—handy for stops, since both feet could be put on the ground while the clutch was disengaged. *Indian 1917 catalog*

ing hype, but the boast revealed Indian's confidence that the Powerplus couldn't be bested by Harley-Davidson or Excelsior. The Powerplus engine became the nucleus of Indian success from 1916 to the end of production in 1953.

The 61ci Powerplus had a smaller bore and longer stroke than the F-head, the new job measuring $3^{1}/_{8} \times 3^{31}/_{32}$in. At the time, popular theory was that a long stroke improved torque, so Indian advertisements emphasized this point. The cylinder heads were one-piece iron castings with removable caps above each valve. To ease cold weather starting problems, priming cups were built into the cylinder heads, enabling the rider to inject gasoline with a syringe.

Although the parts were different, the Powerplus valvetrain bore the same layout as the earlier F-heads, with four valves actuated by a single camshaft with two cams. The engine-driven timing gear was moved from the crankcase to the timing case. The Powerplus webbed flywheels were another

Year and model .... 1917, 1918 and 1919 Light Twin, Type O	Year and model .... 1918 Powerplus twin-cylinder
Engine .... side-valve horizontally opposed twin, outside flywheel	Engine .... side-valve 42 degree V-twin
Bore and stroke .... 2x2½ in.	Bore and stroke .... 3⅛x3³¹/₃₂ in.
Displacement .... 15.7 ci, 257.3 cc	Displacement .... 60.88 ci, 997.6 cc
Bhp 4	Bhp 18
Lubrication .... wet sump with auxiliary hand pump	Lubrication .... total loss
Ignition .... magneto	Ignition .... magneto
Gearbox ... three-speed, hand-acutated, sliding-gear type	Gearbox ... three-speed, hand-actuated, sliding-gear type
Clutch .... dry	Clutch .... dry
Primary drive .... single-row chain under stamped metal dust cover	Primary drive ...... single-row chain under stamped metal dust cover
Wheelbase .... 49½ in.	Wheelbase .... 59 in.
Wheels and tires .... 21 in. wheels, 21x2.25 tires (catalog reference is 26x2.25 measured across tire dia.)	Wheels and tires .... 22 in. wheels, 22x3.00 tires (catalog reference is 28x3.00 measured across tire dia.)
Suspension ... front, 1917: coil spring cushion cartridge front, 1918: leaf spring; rear, 1917 and 1918 rigid	Suspension .... front, leaf spring fork; rear, optional swinging arm and leaf spring, or rigid
Weight .... 250 lb. (est.)	Weight .... 410 lb. (serviced)
Seat height .... 1917, 29½ in.—1918-1919, 29 in.	Seat height .... 31 in.
Mpg .... 80 (claimed)	Mpg .... 35 (est.)
Oil consumption .... 250 miles/qt.	Oil consumption .... at 30 mph, 400 miles/qt.; at 50 mph, 100 miles/qt.
Top speed .... 45 mph	Top speed .... 60 mph (est.)

design carryover from the F-heads. Single-cylinder 33 ci engines were optional.

As in the F-heads, the connecting rods' big ends turned on roller bearings. A change from F-head practice was the fitting of roller bearings to the pinion (right side) shaft, while the drive (left side) shaft was supported by a plain bearing as in the F-heads. Many F-head parts were carried over into the Powerplus, including the complete

A 1918 Powerplus. Up-down gearshift motion was introduced in 1917 to replace fore-aft motion. Double gold and single black striping were used in 1917, 1918 and 1919. Restoration by Marv Baker.

transmission, clutch, frame, fenders, tanks and handlebars. Gone, however, was the famous Hedstrom concentric carburetor. In its place was the less expensive and conventional Schebler carburetor.

Following British practice, Indian introduced a two-stroke lightweight in 1916, called the Featherweight. These proved unreliable and hard to sell, so they were marketed for only one year. The Feather-weights are rare birds; only five or six examples have been reported.

A number of improvements were incorporated in the 1917 Powerplus twins and singles. The pistons and cylinder barrels were lengthened a quarter inch to provide greater bearing surface, and the piston pin was lowered below the piston center to reduce noisy side slap. New valve caps had

---

Riding a 1918 Powerplus

With a 1913 F-head twin ride behind you, the Powerplus isn't novel. A couple of welcome changes are the three-speed transmission and foot clutch, which make getting off the mark a lot easier. Actually, the foot clutch wasn't a Powerplus innovation, as that feature was provided on some of the later F-heads.

The Powerplus continued to feature a back-up hand clutch, now logically moved to the right side for operation in conjunction with the left-hand throttle. The auxiliary hand clutch was necessary for starting up hills, as there was no handbrake to prevent rolling backward, so one foot was occupied with the brake pedal while the other foot maintained balance.

The Powerplus valve gear is enclosed, so you expect less mechanical noise. The engine should stay cleaner without the constant emission of oil vapor around the inlet valves, as on the F-heads.

The handlebars are uncluttered by the F-head rods, bellcranks and universal joints—a practical improvment, but one that seems to rob mystique from the machine. Out back, there remains the swinging arm rear suspension that was years ahead of its time. The lines are antique, but technically the Powerplus wasn't that far away from bikes of the late 1940s. There's a sense of ruggedness to the Powerplus that was missing from the F-head. You note, however, that the wheel rims are still the bicycle type, the so-called clincher rims that didn't take advantage of tire pressure to hold the rubber against the rim. A running flat on one of these is the same bad news as on the earlier F-heads—the tire can come off the rim, which likely will catapult the rider onto the road.

With your study completed, you're ready to ride. You fire up the Powerplus, and as the motor warms up you confirm that the F-head thrashing of exposed valve gear is a thing of the past. It was progress, of course, but as a collector instead of a rider of seventy years ago, you kind of miss all the F-head racket.

Combined with the antique clutch design, the old sliding-gear setup makes getting into low a noisy operation. With the Powerplus now in low gear, you find there isn't all that delicate easing away of the clutch as on the single-speed F-head. Under way, the feel is similar to the F-head twin, but the Powerplus lives up to its name. If you climb off an F-head and then take a turn on a Powerplus, you can appreciate the added power of the later model. There's also a softer feel to the power impulses of the side-valve Powerplus.

The rocker clutch is handy when getting ready for a stop; you just think about stomping the toe pedal down, and worry later about getting away after you're all set at the stop. Gradually, you find your clutch feel improving so it's possible to slip the clutch accurately. You can even go around a tight corner without downshifting, and the old Powerplus doesn't complain.

You try your hand at shifting. There's a certain charm to mastering the timing of gear-shifts on a sliding-gear transmission. You aren't that good at it on the first couple of shifts, but you begin to improve; gradually, you manage to shift into second gear silently. Shifting into low works best if the bike is rolling along slowly. There's a nice feel to the gears that you get with these old boxes.

Your ride completed, you try to sum up the experience. Here, you muse, are the antique looks of the F-head but with a little more practicality. You label the Powerplus the youngest of Indians that are purely antiques.

---

radiating cooling fins. The fuel tank was redesigned to a simpler shape to increase capacity. On the side of the tank, a new gearshift lever with up and down motion resulted in more direct action to the transmission. The new triple stem fork had additional upper bracing.

Indian continued their lightweight efforts with a tiny 16 ci opposed twin replacing the Featherweight two-stroke. Perhaps inspired by the British-built Douglas, the Model O had the unfortunate nickname of Model Nothing. These little twins were noted for their sewing machine smoothness; however, there proved to be no market for a lightweight, and the Model O was sold in 1917, 1918 and 1919. In 1918, push-pull wire controls replaced the traditional push-pull rods and bellcranks on all Indians.

1919-1924

From 1919 until the end of Powerplus production in 1924, Powerplus changes were minimal due to World War One and engineer Charles B. Franklin who next turned his attention to the design of two new models, the Scout and the Chief. Because of the importance of these models, they'll be treated in later chapters. Our chronology moves on to the mid-twenties, a time when Franklin was finding as much success on the racetracks as in the showrooms with the newly launched Scout and Chief lines.

1925-1928

In 1925 Franklin was busy with racing development along two lines. Following British and European trends, he was experimenting with a new series of 45 ci, 750 cc four-valve overhead twins to replace the old eight-valve 61 ci overheads. Concurrently, he must have surprised himself with the power he'd been able to extract from the 61 ci side-valve design that supposedly was unsuitable for racing. These Franklin side-valve racers had become the front-line troops in the racing war with Harley-Davidson, and continued success in this matchup was especially rewarding in that the road model Indians were of the same general layout.

One of these side-valve Indians was timed at 117 mph on Australia's Sellick Beach in 1925—less than 2 mph slower than the official world's record for a 61 ci, 1000 cc overhead-valve British Brough Superior.

Franklin's first 21 ci, 350 cc side-valve roadster of 1925 was too much akin to its

A circa 1925 Powerplus racer. Restoration by Stephen Wright. *Sam Hotton*

A 1925 Indian Prince. Wedge-shaped tank followed English practice, but proved unpopular in the United States. *Indian 1925 catalog*

British inspiration. The Prince wedge-shaped fuel tank didn't go over well in the United States and was replaced in 1926 by a Scout-styled tank. Judging from the relative popularity of this Indian Prince and the rival Harley-Davidson 21 ci singles among today's collectors, Harley must've sold more of this type than did Indian.

The final Prince appeared in 1928 with a still more shapely fuel tank which it shared with the new Scout Model 101. During the production run, a few overhead-valve Princes were built, enabling Indian to enter these in so-called stock racing events against the Harley Peashooter. Franklin also built at

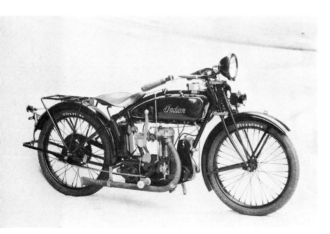

A 1926 Prince. English styling influenced the selection of the girder front fork. Earlier English-patterned wedge-shaped tank has given way to the American-style tank. *Indian archives/Bob Finn*

least four overhead-cam Prince prototypes. One engine was seen in California in the late seventies.

Princes of any configuration are rare in today's antique motorcycle show circuit, much more so than the rival Harley-Davidson singles. A helpful point for collectors is the similarity of many Prince parts with the later 30 ci, 500 cc twin.

Rarer still are the few remaining 45 ci, 750 cc overhead-valve specials designed by Franklin. Only twenty-six of these motors were built in 1926, about half going into racers and half into hillclimbers. Kept out of the international record book by politics, the Franklin overheads were probably the fastest motorcycles in the world. Less than half a dozen Franklin overheads have been spotted at meets in the past twenty years, however. Owning one calls for machinist skills, since some spares don't exist. On the plus side, the Franklin overheads used the Power-plus transmission, clutch and a number of other components.

Ownership and prospects
1901-1915 F-head single and twin

You should be able to keep a 1901-1915 F-head single or twin for ten or more years, using it for the occasional club event, and then turn a modest or perhaps even a significant profit in real dollars. As previously noted, the Hendee and Hedstrom motorcycles are eligible for HCCA events, the termination of the F-heads in 1915 coinciding with HCCA eligibility. Face it, car people are wealthier than motorcycle people. The proximity of the purely collectible founders' bikes to the antique car movement will tend to raise the upper boundary of motorcycle prices that most of us are willing to pay. Incidentally, in the past ten years F-head prices—not adjusted for inflation—have tripled, so this amounts to a true return on investment of about fifty percent when inflation is considered. Although I believe that the biggest F-head money has already been made, I think the F-heads are still good investments.

Already, you can expect to pay about a ten percent differential for a 1915 Indian F-head, as compared to an identically conditioned 1916 Powerplus, and perhaps a fifteen percent differential compared to the 1917 and later Powerpluses. You can expect this price differential between the HCCA eligibles and ineligibles to widen over the years, my guess being a rise of another ten percent in real dollars over the next twenty years. In other words, by the year 2008 I predict that F-heads in general will cost twenty to twenty-five percent more than Powerpluses in general. This prediction could be undone in the unlikely event that HCCA rules are changed, or if Powerplus enthusiasts develop their own organization to nurture Powerplus status.

The total restoration investment for an F-head will vary widely, depending on age. For the 1901–1904 singles with rigid front fork, the sky may be the limit, since with these you're into the status game in which the rules say the earlier the better. Expect the 1905–1908 singles to require a gradually declining total investment, falling to somewhere around fifty percent of the actual dealer's price of the current Harley-Davidson FLHTC for a 1908 or 1909 diamond-framed single. A first-year twin of 1907 may require a premium investment, my guess being about 125 percent of the actual dealer's price of the reference new Harley-Davidson.

For 1908 and later models, twins are much more popular than singles despite the latter's rarer status. Therefore, the rarer singles can usually be purchased at lower prices than the twins. Restoration cost of a single is about the same as for a twin, so a post-1908 single is a riskier investment than a twin of the same year.

The following cost ranges are estimated in relation to the actual dealer's price of the reference new Harley-Davidson. Remember that these figures are provided only as a general guide, since the value of any antique motorcycle is a function of unique circumstances such as documented history, condition and accessory equipment. The circumstances of the buyer and seller will also greatly influence the purchase price.

1909 first-year loop-frame single, eighty percent

1909 first-year loop-frame twin, 100 percent

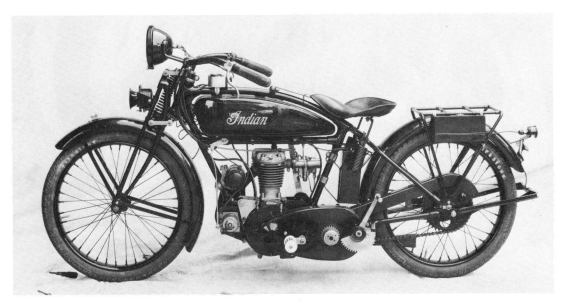

A 1926 Prince. Cost-cutting changes included chain primary drive with sheet metal cover and non-unit construction of the engine and transmission package. *Indian archives/Bob Finn*

1910-1915 one-speed single, seventy-five
  percent
1910-1915 two-speed single,
  seventy-five percent
1910-1915 one-speed twin, ninety
  percent
1910-1915 two-speed twin, ninety
  percent
1915 three-speed single, last F-head,
  seventy-five percent
1915 three-speed twin, last F-head,
  115 percent

Ownership of an F-head Indian is not a casual undertaking. Spare parts are exceedingly hard to come by, and you'll have to be neck deep in the Antique Motorcycle Club of America in order to make the contacts you'll need to scout out what few spares can still be found. More likely, you'll need to develop some restoration skills and establish a parts bin for yourself, things that will give you influence with fellow collectors. Otherwise, paying the going commercial rates for machine shop work will cost you a bundle.

1916-1925 Powerplus single and twin

The 1916-1925 Powerplus Indians have the full antique flavor of the earlier F-heads, plus extra power, a cleaner engine due to the enclosed valves, and greater reliability for cruising in the 40-50 mph range. As with the F-heads, the Powerplus total-loss oiling means serious touring deserves some thought. You should limit your rides to a couple of hundred miles, carry extra oil, or have faith in modern oils. On the latter

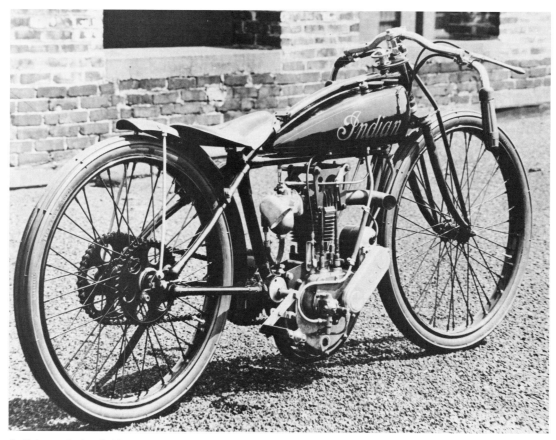

A Prince-derived 30.50 ci, 500 cc flat-track racer. Most Prince racers were the 21 ci, 350 cc versions using the same frame. Princes and

Harley-Davidson Peashooters were racing staples of the 1920s. *Indian archives/Emmett Moore*

point, single viscosity sixty-weight oil is desired but difficult to buy. For typical club runs, at 100 miles or less at 40 mph or less, any good modern oil should suffice, preferably single viscosity and forty to sixty weight.

The clincher wheel rims are another concern, as a running flat can result in a tire completely separating from the rim.

Compared to the F-heads, you should get some kind of price break because the Powerplus models don't qualify for the HCCA events. Of course, on the selling end, you'll probably have to give somebody else a price break too. This is how things should be, but in practice it's hard to see any difference in prices of most later F-heads compared to most Powerpluses. With the exception of the 1915 models, F-heads were one- or two-speed bikes, a point which leads some buyers to prefer the three-speed Powerpluses.

All in all, there should be less upward price pressure on the Powerpluses than on the F-heads. Still, you should break even on a Powerplus investment. Ballpark estimates to total restoration investment, compared to the actual dealer's price of the Harley-Davidson FLHTC, are sixty percent for 1918–1925 Powerplus singles and 100 percent for 1918–1925 Powerplus twins. Add another five percent for a 1916, last year of the wedge-shaped tank as used on F-heads. Add another three- percent for 1917, last year of the rods and cranks handlebar controls.

1916 Model K Featherweight
1917–1918 Model O Light Twin

Only three of the 1916 Model K Featherweight singles have been publicly displayed during the past twenty years. One Featherweight is in California, one is in Pennsylvania, and one is in Michigan. Michigan and British Columbia are the homes of the only confirmed complete Model O Light Twins. Accordingly, the investment potential of these motorcycles can't be predicted.

1925–1928 Prince side-valves and
overhead-valves

These 1925–1928 Prince side-valves and overhead-valves are fun bikes at organized rallies, offering something different for Indian fans used to V-twins. But rarity doesn't offset the bad points of these motorcycles. Prince performance is no better than later lightweights which are more maintainable. Cruising speeds of 35–40mph limit them to local rides. Parts will be a problem, too. The Harley-style stamped sheet-metal

A 1926 45ci overhead-valve racer. The front oil pump supplies oil to the base of the front cylinder; the rear cylinder gets its oil from the crankshaft oil sling. Four 1926 road racers were built, two for California dry-lakes racing and two for Europe. Restoration by Chuck Vernon.

A 1926 factory-prepared hill climber. Overhead-valve racers and hill climbers featured 16:1 compression ratio and burned methyl alcohol. Restoration by Chuck Vernon.

Year and model	1928 Prince
Engine	side-valve single
Bore and stroke	$2\frac{3}{4} \times 3^{37}/_{64}$ in.
Displacement	21.25 ci 348 cc
Bhp	6 (est.)
Lubrication	total loss
Ignition	magneto
Gearbox	three-speed, hand-acutated, sliding-gear type
Clutch	dry
Primary drive	single-row chain under stamped metal dust cover
Wheelbase	54 in.
Wheels and tires	19 in. wheels, 19x3.30 tires (Optional, 18x3.00) (catalog reference is 25x3.30 or 24x3.00 measured across tire dia.)
Suspension	front, girder fork; rear, rigid
Weight	272 lb. (serviced)
Seat height	28 in.
Mpg	55 (est.)
Oil consumption	200-400 miles/qt., depending on speed
Top speed	60 mph (est.)

primary chain cover was an uncharacteristic Indian retreat from progress, and an embarassment to Indian fans.

The overhead-valve Prince had an honorable history in dirt-track racing, but Prince overheads are too rare to be predictable. Perhaps California isn't representative, but for what it's worth, in ten years of California antique bike show, I've seen only one overhead-valve Prince and no side-valve versions. All this adds up to a lack of practicality that's not balanced by mystique. Hooray for the people who restore them and show them, but I'm sure they consider theirs a labor of love.

The estimated restoration investment, compared to the actual dealer's price of the Harley-Davidson FLHTC, is forty percent for the side-valve version and forty-five percent for the overhead-valve version.

1908–1931 Racers and hillclimbers

There aren't enough of the early Indian competition bikes around to establish any kind of meaningful statistical base. Of the original dozen or so big-base eight-valve twins, only one is a confirmed survivor in the eastern United States, and another is rumored to exist in Australia. From eight to ten small-base eight-valve twins are believed to exist, joined by twelve to fifteen small-base four-valve singles. About eight to ten of the 1920 Daytona Powerplus racers—with big exhaust elbows—are thought to exist, along with about a dozen of the 1919–1922 regular Powerplus hillclimbers. Of the late Franklin 45ci overheads, perhaps ten are still around. Thus, there's no rating for the early racers. For those few who collect the old racers, nothing else will do, but you're forewarned that high prices and the limited opportunities to ride these all-or-nothing beasts are going to make these a hard sell down the road. Growth value is unpredictable because the mold is not completely set for this narrow market. The cost to purchase and restore early racers varies, and is not predictable.

Chapter 2

Scouts and Chiefs 1920-1939

★★★	1920-1928 Scout
★★★	1922-1931 Chief
★★★★	1928-1931 Model 101 Scout
★★–★★★	1932 Chief
★★	1932-1941 Scout Pony, Junior Scout and Thirty-fifty
Not ratable	1933 Motoplane
★★★	1933-1939 Chief
★★★	1934-1939 Sport Scout

History
1920-1923

Charles B. Franklin's greatest designs were the mid-sized Scout and the large Chief, both side-valve V-twins. The 37 ci, 600 cc Scout came on the scene in late 1919 as a 1920 model, and was an instant commercial success. Scout reliability was a strong point, giving rise to the factory slogan, "You can't wear out an Indian Scout." Indian riders expanded this to a chant: "You can't wear out an Indian Scout, or its brother the Indian Chief. They're built like rocks to take hard knocks; it's the Harley's that cause the grief."

Scout power was surprising. A Scout set a twenty-four-hour world's road record in 1920, covering 1,114 miles over a closed

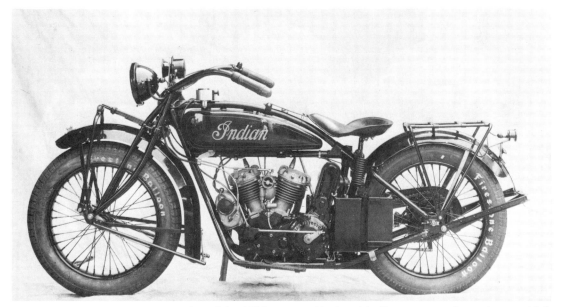

This 1926 Scout 37 is representative of the 1920 through early 1928 models. The box on the tank top contains the light switch and ammeter. The vertical rod is the compression release which lifts the exhaust valve during starting. *Indian archives/Bob Finn*

Year and model	1920 Scout
Engine	side-valve 42 degree V-twin
Bore and stroke	2¾x3⅛₆ in.
Displacement	36.4 ci (referred to as 37 ci), 596 cc
Bhp	11
Gearbox	three-speed, hand-actuated, sliding-gear type
Wheelbase	54½ in.
Wheels	20 in. (catalog reference was 26 in. but included tire dia.)
Tires	20x3.00 (catalog called this 26x3.00)
Suspension	front, leaf spring; rear, rigid
Weight	serviced, 340 lb.; dry, 315 lb.
Seat height	28 in.
Mpg	50 (est.)
Top speed	55 mph (est.)

A 1926 Scout 37. Tire options were Goodyear or Firestone. Crankcases were painted to match frame, fenders and tank. The small circular protrusions in the middle of the cylinder heads are the priming cups. *Indian archives/Bob Finn*

course in Australia. This was 250 miles more than the previous record held by a 61 ci motorcycle.

Following on the heels of the tremendously popular Scout came Franklin's next creation, the 61 ci, 1000 cc Chief. The Chief was originally billed as a big Scout, with emphasis given to the Chief's sidecar suitability. When the first Chiefs came out as 1922 models, the companion Powerplus 61 had been on the market for six years. Compared to the Powerplus, whose frame had roots back in 1909, the 1922 Chief was a compact motorcycle, and was hailed as such by the motorcycle press. Even the choice of a 61 ci engine was considered avant-garde, as

A 1926 Chief with sidecar. Indian stressed the Chief as a sidecar hauler, and for that reason the kickstarter was on the left. The kickstarter was moved to the right side on the 1932 Chiefs, but throughout production the starter was reversible. *Indian archives/Bob Finn*

other makers had been toying with larger motors.

A retrograde step was the abandonment of the cradle spring frame. (On the Scout this could've been justified as an economy measure.) Apparently, the cradle spring frame was considered too unconventional in appearance for the conservative motorcycle public. Moreover, Excelsior and Harley-Davidson had done a good job of convincing riders that the cradle spring frame caused broken chains.

Only minor changes were implemented from 1921 through 1923, in both the Scout 37 and the Chief 61. The 61 ci Chief was joined by the 74 ci Big Chief in the 1923 line-up.

The Scout grabbed more publicity than the Chief. The smaller model broke both the Canada-to-Mexico and transcontinental records in 1923, records previously made on a 61 ci Excelsior V-twin and an 80 ci Henderson four. Several hundred Scouts were placed in police service in Massachusetts and Pennsylvania, a surprising development in view of the previous preference for larger motorcycles. All Indians got a new fork in 1924, the previous push-action fork giving way to a pull-action fork.

The famous Indian helical gear primary drive introduced on the 1920 Scout remained an Indian selling point from 1920 through 1933. The drive was noisy, but would outlast the motorcycle. *Indian 1925 catalog*

With the Scout and Chief, we start moving away from the antique mystique and toward growing practicality. Unlike the rivals, the Scout and Chief were integrated designs instead of collections of bits and pieces. In both motorcycles, the engine and transmission were bolted together, and connected by an indestructible helical-gear primary drive operating in a cast-aluminum oil bath case. Thus, the package was a true

By the late teens the sidecar had already lost out to the automobile in the battle for basic transportation dollars. Things were different in Europe, where sidecars flourished until the mid-1950s. *Indian archives/Bob Finn*

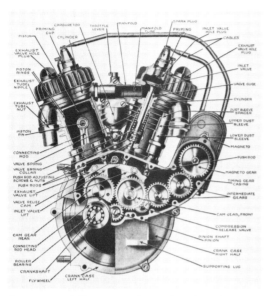

Cutaway of Scout engine, showing the two-camshaft layout, one cam for each cylinder. The Chief engine was an enlarged version. *Indian 1925 catalog*

powerplant, which eliminated the messy and time-consuming chore of primary chain adjustment. On other motorcycles, that had their transmission mounted to the frames,

primary chain adjustment also dictated adjustment of the rear chain. Two forward mounts on either side of the engine and one aft mount on the gearbox, firmly secured the powerplant into a double-loop cradle frame.

Engine layouts were likewise identical on the Scout and Chief. Scouts and Chiefs used two camshafts, one for each cylinder. Each camshaft had only one cam lobe, the cam doing double duty by operating both intake and exhaust valves of one cylinder. Actuation was by means of a pair of bellcrank valve lifters. The front cylinder cam gear spun a train of three gears, the third gear turning the magneto.

The cylinders and cylinder heads were of the Powerplus style: one-piece iron castings with removable caps above each valve. Roller bearings were fitted to the connecting rod big end, and to both the drive and pinion shafts. The flywheels were of one-piece webbed construction, the outer rim of each flywheel encircling a beam that was drilled for crankshaft and mainshaft installation. The Scout bore and stroke were $2^3/4$ x $3^1/16$in. The Chief 61 bore and stroke were $3^1/8$ x $3^{31}/32$in, while the Big Chief 74 measured $3^1/4$ x $4^7/16$in. Where possible, Powerplus parts were

A 1928 101 Scout. Black spokes were standard until 1931. This example is a 37ci, 600cc model. *Goodyear archives/Stephen Wright*

used. For example, the Scout 37 had the Powerplus 61 crankshaft, and the Chief used Powerplus pistons and rings.

With all the technical wizardry of old lawn mowers, these engines stand out as monuments to the American slogan, "There's no substitute for cubic inches." That may seem like an overstatement about the 600 cc Scout, but the British and Continental motorcycle companies considered 500 cc the practical limit for mid-sized bikes. When the foreign firms later began to introduce overhead-valves to their 500 cc models, Indian needed only to enlarge the Scout from 600 to 750 cc to get the same results without the teething troubles experienced across the Atlantic.

No question about the Chief, as this was a big motorcycle in the American tradition. The parts in these engines are huge. The valves measure two inches across, the kind of stuff that fits into big old Ford and Chevy engines.

If a Chief bottom end starts to go bad, the rider will usually get plenty of warning.

A 1931 101 Scout shown out of sequence with a purpose. This motorcycle was newly restored in the mid-1970s without the battery box and proper toolbox as shown in the previous photo. Since then, it's become possible to purchase replica items. *George Hays*

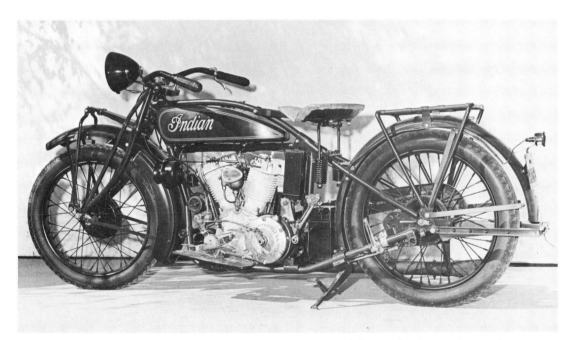

A 1928 Chief owned by motorcycle historian and *Iron Redskin* author Harry V. Sucher. Original crankcases and primary drive were painted to match frame, fenders and tank. Restoration by Ernest Skelton. *George Hays*

These engines have been known to run several thousand miles with gradually noisier knocking before the big bang. As far as life expectancy, you can figure about 20,000 miles on a top end job and about 35,000 miles on the bottom end.

The clutch, however, is perhaps the strongest component of both models, and in fact it's possible to tow a car behind a Chief. Because the clutch runs in an oil bath, the mechanism will outlast the rest of the motorcycle provided the rider keeps oil in the primary case. A Scout or Chief can be left running curbside, in gear with the clutch disengaged, for an hour or so—or until the motor burns up—and the clutch will not fry. The clutch was a good selling point for dealers trying to win police business.

Now for the bad part. Indian wet clutches *more or less* work, whether new or with

A 1928 Chief. Behind the oil cap can be seen the auxiliary oil hand pump for supplementing the engine-driven pump during rough going. Behind the hand pump is the gas cap with removable syringe for priming the cylinders with gasoline. Next in line is the gas shutoff, then the compression release. *George Hays*

100,000 miles behind them. As an item designed in the early 1920s, the clutch is pretty crude. Oil drag, even on a new unit, means putting the Chief into low is a process of jerking the gears into mesh, in order to avoid prolonged grinding. This happens on the Scouts, too, but the Chiefs are worse because of the extra torque that grinds. This was overcome in 1952 by the fitting of a clutch brake, a device which would hold the driven-plates motionless.

The major problem with the Chief clutch begins after a few miles, when the clutch becomes grabby. When the clutch gets hot, say in congested traffic, the plates become glazed. The result is that in the last moments of engaging the clutch, the slick glaze is overcome suddenly, and the rider is greeted with a rough and noisy crunch. This doesn't hurt the motorcycle, but it is annoying, especially when you stall at a traffic light. On the Scout, the rider can feel this too, but it never seems to get as out of hand as on the Chief.

Scout and Chief transmissions were similar to the Powerplus design. On the Scouts and Chiefs the transmission housings were engine-mounted instead of frame-mounted as on the Powerplus. Unlike the Powerplus models, which had both the primary and final drives on the left side, the Scouts and Chiefs had a crossover layout with left-side primary and right-side final drive. Commonality was a goal, however, so the Powerplus triple gear and sliding gear and a few other parts show up in the Chief gearbox.

Lights are pretty good on Scouts and Chiefs, aided by the use of a modern battery. As for real Indian batteries, they're long gone, but early models have a battery box that hides a modern replacement. On later models, a modern battery can be hidden under a trick fiberglass cover that looks just like the original Indian battery.

Generator belt adjustment is important. For 1932 and later Chiefs and Standard Scouts, and for Scouts (except with 101 frame) the generator is clamped onto the vertical frame tube behind the transmission, and belt adjustment is accomplished by moving the generator either up or down on the tube. All well and good, except that the

A 1929 Model 101 Scout. Longer wheelbase and lower frame resulted in near perfect handling, as the 101 was both stable and agile. The 101 was favored by carnival trick riders for years. As late as 1987 a 101 Scout was in such use in Germany.

generator is also free to move left and right. Accurate alignment of the generator pulley and the engine-driven pulley can be achieved by carefully using a straightedge. A properly installed generator belt will last about 10,000 miles; an improperly installed belt may fail in less than 500 miles.

Simplified accurate adjustment was provided on the Model 101 Scouts by mounting the generator to a plate that was bolted to the upper frame rails below the saddle. Two parallel slots in the plate provided for anchoring each end of the generator so that it couldn't twist under load. The pre-1932 Chiefs had gear-driven generators mounted forward of the engine beneath the magneto.

On the road, gas consumption with the standard setup can be as good as 50 mpg. Some Indian riders set up their engines for rich running, as a means of keeping the motor a little cooler. Under such conditions, with no headwind and running on level ground, gas mileage can fall to about 35 mpg on a Chief. Typical gas mileage is 35-40 mpg.

Oil consumption on total-loss Indians is a matter of some debate. According to the factory literature of both the Indian and Harley-Davidson companies, oil consumption should vary widely, depending on average speed. At an average of 30 mph a quart of oil was supposed to last about 400 miles; cruising at 50 mph generally was expected to yield about 125 miles per quart. Conversely, some of today's riders of these old motorcycles claim 200 miles per quart is reasonable oil consumption for 50 to 55 mph cruising. Others never run over 40 mph except for brief spurts, yet believe 150 miles per quart of oil is about right. Speaking for myself, my 1929 Scout averaged about 280 miles per quart for 8,000 miles of mostly 55 mph cruising, before suffering connecting-rod bearing failure.

Considering my Scout mileage, I have to wonder if my Scout was really under-oiled or if the beast was doomed to failure in any case. However, I'm not one to take big risks with my old iron, so my rebuilt 1929 Scout is adjusted for an average of 200 miles per quart for steady 55 mph running. Anyway, you should get somewhere between 100 and 200 miles per quart at 55 mph, depending on the health of your Indian and your willingness to test the limit of lubrication.

Opinions also vary concerning the best oil to use in total-loss motorcycle engines. Some riders recommend any vegetable-based oil, while others suggest any racing oil. The originally recommended oil was a single-viscosity heavy grade, about sixty weight, but sixty-weight oil is no longer generally available. A friend of mine recommends any name-brand single-viscosity oil. He reasons that most Indians are ridden for only a few hundred miles per year, and that most Indian rides are one hour or less; therefore, he believes there's no point in buying expensive oil.

For my 1929 Scout I follow the lead of John Eagles, who has ridden his Scout over 50,000 miles during the past twenty years; we use pure castor bean oil obtained from an industrial supplier. This Standard AA castor oil costs about two times regular automotive oil.

Scout and Chief engines are tough, but they do need routine attention. Although side-valve engines have always had a reputation for reliability, in fact these motors merit closer attention to the valve gear department than do overhead-valve engines. With overhead valves, neglected valve clearances ordinarily result in the clearances opening up, with the worst consequences being a falloff in power and gas mileage. Big side-valvers have no interloping pushrods and rocker arms between cams and valve stems. Without these intermediate parts to absorb wear, it's possible for valve clearances to close up over extended mileage in a side-valve motor. The usual result is burnt

A 101 Scout and owner/restorer John Eagles. Eagles is one of the top 101 Scout technicians, and has put over 56,000 miles on this Scout. The headlight is a nonstandard period piece. Low seating position is apparent.

exhaust valves. Why? Because lack of valve clearance means the valve is early in opening and late in closing, and having spent less time on the seat, the valve conducts less heat away into the cylinder head.

In my own case, I failed to check valve clearances on my 1947 Chief, and at 22,000 miles the front cylinder exhaust valve gave up. Actually, I think the exhaust valve went sour at about 15,000 miles, as the Chief used to start up with compression on only one cylinder. Of all the crazy things, the loosely fitting valve was adequate to hold in the combustion, and with the low revs turned, my Chief soldiered on for another few thousand miles with the problem pending. In any case, before a ride of several hundred miles, the prudent owner will make sure the clearances are set to factory standards, or a couple of thousandths looser.

Scouts and Chiefs that are allowed to go unused for extended periods can suffer in a couple of areas. The electrical system deserves attention; if these motorcycles are only occasionally used, the batteries can weaken. A weekly ride or charge-up will prevent this. A snap-connector can be installed on the battery hot wire to combat battery drainage during prolonged inactivity. Many restorations now include conversion to a twelve-volt electrical system; this helps when you shop for replacement bulbs.

Another problem peculiar to seldom-ridden Scouts and Chiefs is the possibility of "wet sumping." A wet sump occurs when too much oil is in the crankcase, which can happen to an Indian twin that has been parked for several weeks. Oil from the tank tends to drain slowly past the crankcase check valves into the motor. The resulting wet-sump condition forces the motor to expend significant energy acting like a compressor, as the extra oil in the bottom end raises crankcase pressure dramatically. In fact, this can get so bad that the motorcycle will quit running. Again, this is not a problem for a regularly ridden machine. For the infrequent rider, the prevention is the five-

A 101 Scout Bobber. Many riders during the thirties, forties and fifties trimmed bodywork from their motorcycles to produce a type known as Bobbers. Front-end geometry was never changed on Bobbers, as all changes were supposed to improve the function of the motorcycle. Restoration by Dewey Bonkrud.

minute chore of removing the crankcase oil level check plug, and draining the extra oil.

1924-1931

Detail changes were made to the Chief and Scout from 1924 through 1929. Several were very significant. Removeable heads debuted on the 1925 Chief and Scout. A front brake was added in 1928. In 1930 the Chief received a cast-aluminum tank, but this feature was not carried over in 1931. The Scout was treated to two important updates. In 1927, a 45 ci version was marketed alongside the familiar 37 ci model, both configurations using the traditional short Scout frame. The 45 ci version was obtained by increasing the bore from 2¾ to 2⅞ in. and the stroke from 3¹/₁₆ to 3½ in.

In the spring of 1928, the Scout was reshaped into the Model 101 Scout. The wheelbase was stretched from 54½ to 57⅛ in., and the saddle height lowered to 26¼ in. A smaller tank and a more graceful upper frame rail completed the visual improvements. Both 37 and 45 ci versions were offered through the end of 1931.

The Indian company was purchased by E. Paul DuPont in 1930. With his connections, DuPont arranged for the full 1931 Indian line to be treated to a variety of optional one-and two-color finishes in DuPont Duco Lacquer. Chrome plating was first used on small parts in 1930 at the start of DuPont's reign.

A 1931 Chief with cast-aluminum tanks. Cast-aluminum tanks were introduced on the 1930 Chiefs, and existing stocks used up during the 1931 production run before switching back to stamped tanks. Cast tanks never appeared on other Indians. The new headlight mounting system shown here was also used on the 101 and Four.

A 1932 Scout, featuring a Scout 45 engine in the Chief frame. This was the new taller look, following the trend of English and Continental manufacturers. Later Sport Scout barrels and manifold have been installed. Restoration by Dewey Bonkrud.

Representative of the new small twins is this 1933 Motoplane. The 45ci Motoplane was introduced a few months after the debut of the 30.50ci Scout Pony. Engine size and names were the only differences between these models. *Hill/Bentley*

Year and model	1928 Model 101 Scout
Engine	side-valve 42 degree V-twin
Bore and stroke	2⅞x3½ in.
Displacement	45 ci
Bhp	18 (est.)
Gearbox	three-speed, hand actuated, sliding gear
Wheelbase	57⅛ in.
Wheels	18 in. (catalog reference was 25 in. but included tire dia.)
Tires	18x3.85 (catalog called this 25x3.85)
Suspension	front, leaf spring; rear, rigid
Weight	370 lb.
Seat height	26¼ in.
Mpg	50 mph (est.)
Top speed	70-75 mph stock, 85-100 mph with custom cams and porting

A new oil pump was installed in the 1931 twins. This pump was throttle regulated, the idea being to reduce the reliance on the auxiliary hand-operated pump in heavy going. Nevertheless, today's long-time Indian enthusiasts say the 1931 oil pump often provided too much oil under fast riding.

The Model 101 Scout of 1928 through 1931 was never equaled in affection and respect by the later Indians. The late Rollie Free set an American Class C (stock) motorcycle record at Daytona Beach on a 1938 Indian Sport Scout, and had a hand in tuning the Sport Scout of the famous Ed "Iron Man" Kretz. For a decade, Free's specialty was tuning Sport Scouts, the bike that replaced the 101. When I asked Free which was his favorite Indian, I fully expected him to rave about the Sport Scout. I was wrong. Without hesitation, but with much emphasis, Free answered that dollar for dollar, the 101 Scout was the best Indian ever built.

Another pal of Iron Man Kretz was Long Beach, California, Indian dealer Joe Koons, who had accompanied Kretz on his Sport Scout campaigns. Joe's fishing yacht of the 1950s bore the name "One-O-One," twenty-five years after the model went out of production.

The late Red Wolverton, long-time Pennsylvania Harley-Davidson dealer, recalled visiting a motorcycle show in early 1932 with Arthur Davidson. Davidson, one of the four cofounders of Harley-Davidson, looked carefully at Indian's new 1932 Scout, a 45 ci engine in a Chief frame. Then he remarked, "Boy are we glad to see that. That 101 was giving us fits."

1932-1934

Indian made substantial changes in their line-up for 1932. Chiefs received new, taller

A 1934 Sport Scout. The T-shaped manifold would give way to a Y manifold in 1936. Original 1934 Sport Scouts didn't have the hinged rear fender shown. The 1934 Sport Scout cylinders also had parallel head finning like the 101. *Indian 1934 catalog*

The oil bath chain primary drive introduced on the Chief for 1934. The 1934 Sport Scout primary drive was the same in principle, although the parts were different. The chain primary drive was silent, and like the earlier helical gear drive would outlast the motorcycle. *Indian 1938 dealer kit*

Riding a Model 101 Scout

To get some idea of what this is all about, let's take another imaginary ride; this time, the steed will be the Indian 101 Scout "Bobber." I can fix this up with the owner, because that's me.

First comes the sit test. You settle into the seat, and I do mean *into* the seat. You ask me why the seat feels so good. I tell you, because the seat is a half-pan, the leather of the forward section largely conforms to *your* anatomy, not to Joe Average's body. You tell me the bike sure is low to the ground, and I nod. You begin bouncing up and down on the seat, feeling the soft coil springs stretch under load and contract on the upbeat. You place one foot on a floorboard, and then deftly get that foot down and the other one up, and repeat this a couple of times. You twist the grips. You bounce some more. You place both feet firmly on the ground, and comment that your legs are as comfortably bent as though you're sitting in a dining room chair. You lean the Scout to the left and to the right, to the left and to the right, then turn the forks this way and that. A grin breaks out on your face as you tell me you like this. I smile, and say I knew you would.

I let you start the Scout. The drill starts with two priming kicks, with the choke closed, the throttle wide open and the ignition kill button depressed. The old critter kicks over easily. Each upstroke of the kickstarter makes a rackety sound, like a castle drawbridge. You open the choke three notches, position the left-hand throttle at about one-eighth open, position the right-hand ignition control at about three-quarters advanced (that is, three-quarter throttle) and release the kill button. On the next kick, just as advertised, the motor roars to life. The noise is deep, strong and looking for a fight. "Were they all this loud?" you ask. "Well, not quite," I answer.

With your F-head and Powerplus rides behind you, you tell me confidently that left-hand throttles don't bother you at all. I fall for it. You feather the clutch to the tune of considerable noise and are away without apparent difficulty, although you're indeed nervous about riding my pride and joy.

You cruise around the corner, out of sight, and five minutes later, you really get the hang of it. You aren't wild about the left-hand throttle, but shifting the right-hand "jockey" shift lever is a ball. You can actually feel the gears slip into place. And why not? The shift lever operates directly, in other words, without any connecting linkages between the lever and the transmission. What you see is what you get. Shifting from low to second, you feel the sliding of the double gear sideways across the main shaft; you feel the teeth of the sliding gear flirting with the middle set of the triple gears on the jackshaft. You keep a gentle pressure on the lever, and then you feel the gears come into mesh. It's almost sexual.

The Scout feels feather light; fingertips can do the steering. You've been around, so you know that agility and rock-steady stability aren't supposed to happen together. Very well, you tell yourself, a little no-hands action will prove this point. You slow to 30 mph for the big test.

You put both hands in your lap, but you're ready to move fast. The Scout yawns, because it's done this so many times before. Nothing whatsoever happens, except that the two of you keep going perfectly straight ahead. "Well what of it?" you ask, for lots of bikes can do this at 30 mph. You try 20 mph, and it still moves straight and steadily. At 15 mph, the same confidence is there. The Scout's confident and you're confident. At 10 mph, just the slightest weave is apparent, but a little body lean this way, then that way, and you stay in control. Better not push your luck, you tell yourself, but with nothing but knee pressure you steer the Scout around a corner into a side street. "Can I actually come to a complete stop, no-hands?" you wonder. You try it, but at about 5 mph you finally have to grab the bars. The experiment is so much fun that you keep the Scout in second gear for another minute or two for more of this no-hands trolling.

Now to a main road, to the middle rpm, to high gear, and to 45, 50, 55 mph. The exhaust note sounds like a Chief at 70 mph, but the smaller motor is happy with these revolutions. And smell that hot castor oil! Smells like a racetrack. The pavement is smooth, but still its little unseen irregularities feed back through the seat springs and keep you moving gently up and down. Surprise, the leaf spring fork actually does a good job of absorbing the worst of a visibly rough spot.

Now to a dirt road. Ouch! Better relax those forearms, because there isn't enough fork action off the pavement. Here comes a big hole. You put more weight on your feet and pull back on the bars, like you're going to get

continued on page 50

49

continued from page 49

up out of that chair. The fork does a whump and the rear tire does a slam bang. But you're OK, and it didn't hurt a bit. Hey, this is a bigger kick going 20 mph than a modern motocrosser gives at 70 mph.

Here's a paved road again. Darn! Time to get back. You ride back toward my place, with your left hand on the throttle, your right elbow in the middle of your right thigh, your right hand nonchalantly resting on the tank top. You pass a guy on a Honda and he does a double take. You pretend not to notice him, park your left hand on your left knee, and keep steering with almost imperceptible shifts of your body, the two handgrips naked in the wind.

And here you are at my place. You kill the motor. You *have* to ask. I answer, No, it's not for sale.

I bought my 1929 "Bobber" in late 1985. I've put about 8,000 miles on the Scout (I say *about* because for the first year the bike didn't have a speedometer). Most of my riding has been to and from antique motorcycle events, cruising at 55 mph as measured by my companion's calibrated speedometer. About a third of my total mileage was put on in eleven days during the summer of 1987, between Los Angeles and Denver. Gas mileage has averaged out at 50 mpg.

I've found the 101 surprisingly comfortable. After riding eleven or twelve hours per day during my big Colorado adventure, I was fresher than has been my fate with new motorcycles. For pavement riding, the spring seat has more than offset the lack of rear wheel suspension. The limited front fork travel is nevertheless adequate to prevent fatigue at the 55 mph clip.

Performance has been a surprise, too. Those iron cylinder heads and barrels conjure up images of overheating, yet this hasn't been the case even in near-100 degree riding in the deserts of California and Arizona, and at 55 mph too. The motor has a cute, underpowered look because the cooling fins are small, yet the critter is happy to spin fast, hour after hour. For the kind of riding that I do, the 101 performance is on a par with the more impressive looking Indian sequel, the Sport Scout.

For another endorsement of the 101 Scout, I yield to John Eagles. John has been a 101 rider for over thirty years, and has restored and repaired them since 1959.

"My favorite Indian is the 101 Scout from 1929 and 1930. I feel the 101 series was the first motorcycle to be reliable enough to get out and travel on. The 101 had dependability, comfort, and stability. Maybe there were other motorcycles that were as good. The 101, if it's properly geared and properly run, will never wear out. As many of them as are still running around the country kind of proves that.

"The only bad thing about the 101 is the need to carry your own oil. If you carry enough oil to make a long trip, you don't have any room for your luggage.

"I've ridden my 101 several times from California to Durango, Colorado, where my folks live. I've made the same trip on BMWs and on a Honda Gold Wing Aspencade. On the BMWs and the Honda Aspencade both, you get out there and go like hell to make Flagstaff, Arizona, the first night—500 miles. On the 101, you leave early and hold it to about 55 or 60 mph. You ride constantly. And you make Flagstaff the first day.

"So what's the difference? I have to stop and rest—regroup my nerves—more on a high speed machine than I do when riding a more reasonable speed and enjoying the country more. No matter what motorcycle I've made that trip on, I pull into Durango the second day about three o'clock in the afternoon. On the 101, you feel more relaxed just sitting there for long periods of time."

frames which matched up with longer front forks to create a totally different silhouette. Chief and Scout fuel tanks were restyled. The restyling was along the lines of the taller look which began to take over in Britain in 1929.

The historic standard magneto ignition was replaced by standard battery ignition, but without a distributor. Accordingly, a waste spark occurred on the exhaust stroke—both plugs fired every revolution. Magneto ignition was optional.

To the dismay of most Indian fans and dealers, the Model 101 Scout was discontinued. The Scout name was still magical, however, so for 1932 the company made available a Scout motor in a Chief frame, the concoction being mislabeled a Scout. Natu-

Year and model	1932 Scout Pony
Engine	side-valve 42 degree V-twin
Bore and stroke	2½x3¹/₁₆ in.
Displacement	30.07 ci
Bhp	12 (est.)
Gearbox	three-speed, hand-actuated, sliding-gear
Wheelbase	52½ in.
Wheels	18 in., clincher type
Tires	18x3.30
Suspension	front, girder and coil; rear, rigid
Weight	315 lb.
Seat height	27 in.
Mpg	50-75 (est.)
Top speed	70 mph

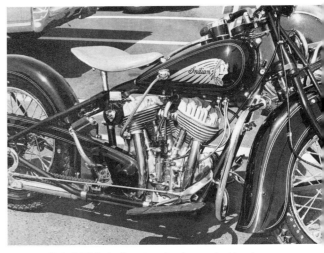

A 1935 Chief. This is the standard paneled tank. The area outlined by the thin double pinstripes could either be the same color as the rest of the tank or could be finished in a contrasting color. This motorcycle has been fitted with the threaded valve dust covers used prior to 1935 and from 1939 on. Original 1935-38 45 ci and 74 ci V-twins were equipped with clip-on covers that were prone to oil leakage. Restoration by Chuck Vernon. *George Hays*

rally, handling of the new Scout wasn't up to 101 standards. Presumably, killing the 101 saved the company money by reducing the variety of components to be manufactured. Some Indian dealers were angry enough to quit.

On the Scout and Chief, lubrication remained total loss. Spring action on the new forks was softer due to wider and thinner spring leaves.

In the spring, about halfway through the model year, a new 30 ci twin-cylinder Scout Pony was added to the 1932 line. Basically, this model consisted of the frame and run-

A 1934 Chief. Although the new Sport Scout featured more stylish fenders, the other 1934 Indians stuck with the earlier fenders as shown here. This was the first year of Indian script on the primary drive cover. The Chief was available with standard A motor or higher performance B motor. The battery is missing in this photo. *George Hays*

Year and model	1934-1939 Sport Scout
Engine	side-valve 42 degree V-twin
Bore and stroke	2⅞x3½ in.
Displacement	45.44 ci
Bhp	stock, 25 (est.); tuned, 28-30 (est.); race-ready, 35-38 (est. for pre-WW II)
Gearbox	standard, three-speed; optional 1937-1939, four-speed or reverse; hand-actuated, sliding-gear type
Wheelbase	56½ in.
Wheels	18 in., drop-center type
Tires	18x4.00
Suspension	front, girder and coil; rear, rigid
Weight	1934-1935 385 lb.; 1936-1937 420 lb.; 1938-1939 440 lb.
Seat height	27 in.
Mpg	55 (advertised)
Top speed	stock 80-85 mph; with custom tuning 90-105 mph

ning gear of a Prince single, mated with the new little side-valve twin-cylinder motor. The gearshift lever was not directly connected to the transmission, as on the 101. Instead, two bellcranks and a push-pull rod were interposed between the rider's hand shift lever and the gearbox. Consequently, the delightful positive feel was gone, and shifting became progressively less precise as wear took its toll on the linkages.

Aimed at the Depression market, the Scout Pony was priced at $225, making it the least expensive American twin. The standard-configuration Scout Pony had floorboards and foot clutch, but an optional sports configuration featured footpegs and hand clutch.

For 1933, the big news was dry-sump lubrication on all the twins. Oil was now continuously circulated between the motor and oil tank. This was a major advance, eliminating the hand pump guess work associated with the old total-loss system when riding fast. Oil consumption was also reduced, so that it was no longer necessary to carry as much extra oil when on long rides. Harley-Davidson didn't fully implement dry-sump lubrication until 1937, so Indian bragged a lot about this feature.

A 1936 Chief, photographed new by owner Joe Sommers. Sommers tuned for Indian racing star Ed Kretz, Sr. Low-speed steering of the leaf-spring Chiefs was on the heavy side, but high-speed stability was outstanding. B motors were now standard, and Y motors were the new hot setup. Tank caps were the new and larger bayonet type. Tail light was new for 1936. *Ed Kretz, Sr.*

Sommers and his Chief. The optional four-speed transmission has a different top section, or shift tower, than the three-speed gearbox. The four-speed ratios were unpopular—low was too low and the other ratios too similar to the three-speed ratios. Also, it was difficult to find neutral in the four-speed. This Chief has the Y motor with larger cooling fins. *Ed Kretz, Sr.*

A companion 45 ci version of the Scout Pony was introduced in 1933 and named the Motoplane. The Motoplane was priced at $250, twenty percent under the 1931 Model 101 Scout price of $310. The 45 ci motor proved too strong for the frame, however, resulting in frame whip. Only a few hundred Motoplanes were built, and the model was not carried over to the following year.

Answering the demand for a true sports model to replace the defunct 101, Indian brought out the 45 ci Sport Scout in 1934. The Sport Scout had the racy English look due to the girder forks and the bolted-up frame, termed a keystone frame by the company. In the keystone frame, the engine and

attaching hardware were used to fill the gap between the front and rear sections of the frame. The keystone frame also gave the motorcycle a light look, although this was more an illusion than a fact: the 1934 Sport Scout weighed 385 lb. according to the catalog, whereas the old 101 Scout was cataloged at 370 lb.

For my money, the Sport Scout keystone frame was a mistake. Across the Atlantic, the old loop-style frame had yielded to the keystone-style frame by the late 1920s. By the time the Sport Scout came out in 1934, the keystone frame was being abandoned by the British and European factories in favor of the cradle frame—exactly the type Charles

B. Franklin had introduced on the original Scout back in late 1919! The bolted-together keystone frame was easy to manufacture and had the deceiving look of lightness. Another plus was the simplicity of adapting the front sections to three-wheelers. Still, the thought of loose frame bolts is worrisome to say the least.

Another undesirable Sport Scout point was the generator setup. Generator drive was by a short chain from the engine, but no provision was made for generator chain lubrication. So it was necessary to remove the chain cover and grease the chain "at regular intervals" according to factory literature (no mileage interval was given). During the short 1942 production run, an engine breather tube was routed to the generator drive for lubrication.

The Sport Scout was graced with new, more streamlined fenders. Another styling highlight was the Indian head motif on the tanks, which would shortly be adapted to the other Indian models and used throughout the 1930s. Meanwhile, the earlier Scout-motor with Chief-frame combination was continued, but the name had changed from Scout to Standard Scout to distinguish this model from the new Sport Scout.

Sport Scout engine dimensions were the same as on the previous Scout. Porting,

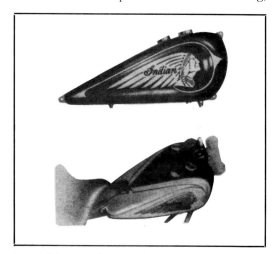

In addition to the standard tank panel design (previously shown), Indian presented two other optional paint schemes for 1935: the Arrow Panel and V Panel. *Indian News*

however, was notably improved as a result of experiments conducted with the cooperation of the famed Massachusetts Institute of Technology.

A comparison of stock Sport Scout valve timing with that of the rival stock Harley-Davidson 45 is illuminating. The Sport Scout used much less valve overlap—the period of time in which both intake and exhaust valves are open—than did the Harley 45. The use of considerable valve overlap in racing engines is well known and justified because of the extreme speed ranges experienced. In touring engines, however, the effectiveness of porting can be gauged by the amount of valve overlap required to produce all-around performance: the more valve overlap required for all-around performance, the less effective are the shapes of the ports and combustion chambers. A look at the specifications is all that's needed to know that the stock Sport Scout was a better breather than the stock Harley 45. Racing results confirmed this, until both factories got seriously involved in racing after a long distinterest. By the late 1930s the performance gap on the tracks had been closed—but not the performance gap on the roads.

On the Sport Scout, the transmission was not bolted to the engine as in the older Scouts and Chiefs. Instead, thick spacer plates joined the motor and gearbox. A Sport Scout styling touch was Indian script on the primary drive cover.

The transmission shift layout was a disappointment. The transmission was shifted indirectly through the bellcrank-and-rod principle dating back to the F-heads, reintroduced by the Prince and made worse by the Scout Pony. On the other hand, transmission reliability would prove as good as the promise; the internal components were all lifted from the Chief. Sport Scout transmissions invariably outlasted the rest of the motorcycle.

In 1934, the famous Indian helical-gear primary drive was not to be found on the Sport Scout or Chief. Indian had switched to primary drive by means of a chain running in a cast-aluminum oil bath case—a four-row chain for the Chief and a three-row chain for the Sport Scout. While this drew criticism from Indian enthusiasts, in practice the oil bath chain drive proved capable of outlasting the motorcycles—which is all that matters— and was less expensive to manufacture. Moreover, the chain setup eliminated the gear whine that some riders found objectionable. Prior to 1932, Harley fans had claimed Indian-mounted police didn't need sirens because the noise was already built-in.

1935

For 1935, the Chief and Standard Scout got new fenders along the lines of the Sport Scout fenders, but with increased valance. A new chainguard was featured on the Chief and Standard Scout. The number of standard optional finishes was reduced to thirteen—think about it, only thirteen standard paint jobs! All 1935 models but the Scout Pony could be purchased with any one of three gas and oil tank trim styles. Rebound springs were added to the leaf spring forks of the Standard Scout and Chief.

The Chief was available with the optional Y motor, which featured larger cylinder cooling fins and aluminum cylinder heads with larger cooling fins. An optional four-speed transmission, larger and longer valve guides, larger and heavier valve springs, new valve dust covers, new roller bearing retainers and a new muffler rounded out the major exclusive Chief updates. The Standard Scout and Chief got a new battery and a new type of quickly detachable rear wheel.

The year 1935 was the last year in which Indian enjoyed a clear styling edge over Harley-Davidson. A 1935 Chief's classic lines appear all the better when parked next to a 1935 Harley. Indians had teardrop-shaped tanks; Harleys had sort of rounded-off

A 1935 45 ci, 750 cc Dispatch Tow. These were used by garages and service stations to pick up cars—provided the car could still move under its own power. The towbar was mounted to the forks and swung down to be connected to the car's rear bumper. After the car was serviced it could be driven back with the motorcycle in tow, then the motorcycle would be unhitched and ridden back to the shop. Indian also built a long Chief-powered Traffic Car three-wheeler with 1,200 lb. carrying capacity. *Indian archives*

In 1936 and 1937, the Chief, Standard Scout and Sport Scout were fitted with these external oil lines servicing the valve guides. Clip-on valve covers with vertical seams made it possible to keep covers and feed lines aligned. *Indian 1937 catalog*

Year and model	1934-1939 Chief
Engine	side-valve 42 degree V-twin
Bore and stroke	3¼x4⁷⁄₁₆ in.
Displacement	73.62 ci
Bhp	40 (est.)
Lubrication	dry sump
Ignition	standard, battery; optional, magneto
Gearbox	standard, three-speed; optional 1935-1939, four-speed or reverse; hand-actuated; sliding gear
Clutch	wet
Primary drive	endless four-row chain, oil bathed, in cast aluminum oil bath case
Wheelbase	61½ in.
Wheels and tires	18 in. drop-center rims, 18x4.00 tires
Suspension	rear, none; front, leaf spring fork
Weight	1933-1934 445 lb. dry; 1935-1937 480-482 lb. dry
Seat height	solo, 29 in., buddy 31.5 in.
Mpg	35-45
Top speed	stock, 85 mph; polished ports and precision ignition timing, 95 mph; with special cams, 100-105 mph

trapezoid, or hump-back, tanks. Just to make it worse, Harley-Davidson put little screws down the middle of the tank. The Indian fenders and chainguard also had a styling flair not found in the Harleys: beginning in 1935, Indian offered three optional paint schemes for the tanks. Indian not only of-

fered more choices of standard colors than Harley, but for $5 extra would supply any color available from DuPont.

A styling point in Harley-Davidson's favor was its front fork, however. Only Indian lovers like me find beauty in the leaf spring fork. The famous British Brough Superior used Harley forks supposedly for their good handling, but my bet is that George Borough just liked the Harley forks for the beauty of their lines.

A technical comparison to a contemporary 1935 Harley-Davidson reveals several points in Indian's favor. Indian offered an optional four-speed transmission; Harley didn't. Indian had dry-sump lubrication; Harley didn't. Indian had reversible throttles, gearshifts, and clutches; Harley didn't. Indian had a cast-aluminum oil bath; Harley didn't. Indian offered optional magneto ignition; Harley didn't. Indian built a lightweight twin; Harley didn't. Indian built a four; Harley didn't. Indian and fifteen years of side-valve motorcycles had set numerous speed records; Harley had six years of side-valve experience and one short-lived side-valve speed record for the stock 45 class, a record that the Indian Sport Scout broke by nearly 10 mph.

Indian had a trailing-link leaf spring fork on their big twin; Harley didn't. Brough

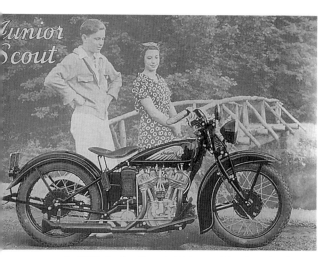

A 1938 Junior Scout. Valanced fenders for the little twin arrived in 1936. *Indian 1938 catalog.*

Riding a 1935 Chief

You listen attentively to the Chief owner explain the ins and outs of the 1935 1200 cc V-twin Indian Chief, his pride and joy. When he's satisfied that you can be trusted, he hands you the keys. The two of you walk over to the Chief, and the owner keeps talking, telling you just what to do, so all you have to do is pay attention. You put the key in the ignition, and swing your right leg over the solo pan seat. Your left hand reaches down to turn on the gas, and to push the choke lever all the way down. Your left foot disengages the clutch, and your right leg quickly comes down on the kickstarter to free the clutch plates. The starter says hello on the upswing with a ratcheting noise. Neat.

You re-engage the clutch with your left foot, and roll on maximum spark retard with the right twistgrip. This Chief is set up the original Indian way, with left-hand throttle and right-hand ignition control, but the owner points out that you have your choice on Indians, many of which were rigged like other motorcycles. You open up the left-hand throttle all the way, and while leaving the ignition off, kick once. You back off about halfway on the right-hand ignition grip, and back the throttle to about one-quarter open. You reach down and bring the choke up three notches. You turn on the key and kick one more time with an "I mean business" thrust, and your reward should be a deep roar. You settle into the seat and enjoy for a few moments the confident feeling imparted by the low seat, which permits your feet to be planted flat on the ground and your legs to be bent at the knees, rather like sitting in a chair. After that, you check that the kickstand is up, give a wave to the owner, jerk the gearshift upward into low and aim.

You renew your acquaintance with old-fashioned horsepower, the stuff that filled the 1918 Powerplus you rode. On this 1935 Chief, the power pulses are still slow enough to be counted when you shift to second at 20 mph, a crunching noise indicating that you didn't do the job right. At 45 mph, you change to high, this time a little more smoothly. The gearshift lever acts directly on the gearbox, like the 101 Scout, and so the same pleasant feel of sliding gears comes through the lever.

Out on an empty two-lane road, the 1935 Chief gives a relaxed, reassuring and regal ride in the 40 to 50 mph range. You ease off the throttle, and keep the speed between 35 and 40 mph for a while. At these speeds, what the British call pottering, you get the feeling that the lazy syncopated lopes belong to a big electrical powerplant engine, or maybe to an old John Deere tractor. While you're pottering—a lost art that deserves to be rediscovered—you feel as if the big iron horse will outlive you and your grandkids.

You are disappointed at the low-speed handling, which is surprisingly heavy. When you turn a corner, the 1935 Chief seems to want to fall into the turn farther than you wish. When you exit the corner, you have to pull the handlebars straight again. Apparently, the new-look frame introduced in 1932 doesn't match up well with the leafspring fork.

You remember some of the owner's words, that although the 1935 Chief puts out only about forty horsepower, it does so at around only 4000 rpm, so each bang brings a lot of punch. Stock gearing on a 74 ci, 1200 cc job is 3.88:1, and is produced with a twenty-three-tooth transmission sprocket.

You confirm the owner's statement that the 1935 Chief runs smoothly with this gearing up to about 50 mph, and then runs roughly until about 60, after which the engine gets on the cam and smoothes out somewhat. You turn up the wick a little more and get into the fast mode at about 66 mph. The Chief exhaust resonates somewhat like the blat of a school bus. Vibration decreases in the handlbars, but increases in the floorboards. At about 68 mph, the Chief really begins to get the shakes, so you back off to the pleasant 66 mph.

At high speeds, the handling is great. The faster you ride the more stable the Chief feels. You jiggle the handlebars to see if the induced wobble will continue; it doesn't. You try this again to make sure, and the results are the same—the Chief insists on holding to a straight course. This is a welcome contrast to old Harleys you've ridden, that tend to keep oscillating once set in motion. You attribute this contrast to the Chief's trailing-link fork action, compared to Harleys' leading-link action.

You ride back to the starting line, where the owner smiles hello. With the motor off, you wax enthusiastically about everything but the vibration. All part of the fun, he says, but adds that there's a cure for the Chief "massage." He says his do-list for today includes changing the

continued on page 58

57

continued from page 57

transmission sprocket, so the bull session continues for about thirty minutes while he replaces the twenty-three-tooth transmission output sprocket with a twenty-five-tooth sprocket.

Back out on the road, you learn the switch to a twenty-five-tooth transmission sprocket has smoothed out things considerably, compared to the stock twenty-three toother, but acceleration is reduced. After slowing to 30 mph for a putt through a town, you find it necessary to spend a lot of time in second gear between traffic lights, and in fact, second gear is now the official town gear. In this traffic, you discover another problem with the taller gearing, the tendency of the Chief clutch to grab. Such is the price of highway smoothness. You conclude the in-between setup, a twenty-four-tooth tranny sprocket, is probably the best for all-around use, and soon you're back out on the highway again, on the open road with all the gear a 74 ci Chief will pack. It's mighty

pleasing to feel the V-twin settled into a steady rhythm at 62 mph.

Oh yes, brakes. You learn there's one good brake, in the back, and it's easy for you to lock up the rear wheel with a strong push on the car-type upright brake pedal. The front brake is something else again. What was it your instructor said? Oh yes, Indian sales literature claimed the front brake was designed to drag rather than to grab. They sure succeeded in their design efforts, you conclude, as you can't imagine ever getting the front stopper to grab. The front brake definitely helps you, but it's mushy, and King Kong himself might find it impossible to lock up the front wheel on pavement.

All too soon, the 1935 Chief and you are rounding that familiar corner, then pottering down the street in second gear, and into the driveway where the adventure began. In the post-ride bull session, your enthusiasm is the reward for the owner's efforts.

Superior couldn't have selected Harley-Davidson leading-link forks for any functional advantage except low-speed handling, as a worn Harley leading-link fork will produce the grandaddy of all high-speed wobbles, while a worn Indian trailing-link fork still steers steadily.

1936-1939

In 1936, a new type of battery and coil ignition became standard. The new battery ignition featured an Auto-Lite distributor. Indian advertising made a big deal out of having a distributor, just the opposite of Harley-Davidson, which bragged about their battery ignition system *excluding* the distributor. Magneto ignition remained optional. A new oil pump featured greater capacity and a removable screen. Detail improvements were made to the pistons and rings. Cosmetically, the previous screw-on tank caps were replaced by larger bayonet caps. A streamlined, flush-mounted taillight completed the minimal styling changes. The Standard Scout was renamed the Scout 45.

During this period, Indian used the so-called trench head on Chiefs. If a cylinder head were held in the palm of the hand, a v-shaped trench of about one-half inch depth

could be observed. The trench separated the valve area from the cylinder bore area, and served to increase combustion turbulence. The trench heads gave better acceleration from low and from medium speeds, but didn't breathe as well at higher speeds. The trench heads are rare today, so apparently this was a short-run experiment.

For 1937, Indian gave in to styling demands and moved the gearshift lever from the crotch position to the front of the tanks. This change introduced an intermediate push-pull rod and bellcrank to the Chief and Scout 45, and robbed riders of the precision feel of the earlier direct-acting shift mechanism in these models. The Sport Scout, which already had indirect shift linkage, had even less direct action after moving the shift lever forward. The Chief got a larger and more graceful chainguard, and the Sport Scout fenders got the full valance of the Chief and Scout 45. The Chief and Scout 45 (with Chief frame) featured interchangeable front and rear wheels.

One 1936-1937 Chief improvement didn't work out. External oil lines were run from the right-hand crankcase to the valve guides, but these resulted in excessive oil mist on the engine's exterior. The reason for the experiment was that Indian V-twins' valve guides were lubricated by crankcase pressure, which was not always effective. A crankcase disc and flutter-valve with a small center hole regulated crankcase pressure. The valve opened on the downstroke, allowing only a small amount of pressure to escape through the center hole, then closed on the upstroke to keep the crankcase vacuum from being excessive. The key to proper operation was selecting the proper size center hole in the disc valve; the slower the average running, the larger the hole. Consequently, there was a tendency for the V-twins to either under-oil the internals or deposit oil mist on the external surfaces, since widely varying speeds weren't ideally

accommodated by the fixed flutter-valve arrangement.

On the 1938 Chief, a new smoother cam case cover wrapped up and around the valve covers. The new cover, however, echoed valve noise, collected dirt and made part of the carburetor mounting hardware inaccessible. Chief forks got a so-called protector shield, which added to the generally cleaner lines.

Engineering changes for 1938 were aimed at cooler running, as constantly improving roads were resulting in a steady increase in sustained riding speeds. Cylinder-head cooling fins on the Sport Scout and Chief were substantially enlarged, and a new oil pump featured still higher capacity plus a new gear-driven return pump. The ignition distributor drive was combined with the oil pump.

A new World's Fair two-color paint scheme was introduced in 1939. Additional chrome plating was another 1939 theme, and was included on the new rear bumper, new

A 1938 Chief engine, showing the new oil pump which incorporated the distributor drive, although the drive opening is blanked off here on this magneto-equipped model. The new smooth cam-case cover wrapped over the crankcase and shrouded the valve covers. Cylinder and cylinder head patterns with large cooling surfaces were standard in 1938 and 1939, optional in 1936 and 1937. Nickel-plated cylinders were standard. This was the last year of the clip-on valve covers. *Indian 1938 dealer sales kit*

A 1938 Sport Scout engine. The Y manifold was introduced in 1936. Nickel-plated cyinders were standard. Behind the motor can be seen the plates which joined the motor and transmission. High-performance Scout and Chief motors were now called Daytona motors in honor of Ed Kretz's victory in the 1937 Daytona 200. *Indian 1938 dealer sales kit*

upswept tailpipe and new air cleaner. Functionally, the only 1939 Chief change was a softer action in the leaf spring fork. The Sport Scout fork links' neutral angle was changed from downward to horizontal.

To defend the honor of the Sport Scout, I turn the words over to Dewey Bonkrud. Bonkrud used to start his Indian in the Wisconsin winter just to listen to the motor! In 1931, when nineteen, he headed for California where he could ride every day of the year.

"My favorite Indian is the fastest one, the Bonneville Sport Scout. It's a thrill to ride it because it does the job so well. You can beat it real hard and it takes it, while giving you every success. But you can't just take one Indian and do the complete job, because for different conditions each model has its own strengths.

"The Sport Scout I rode from California to Springfield, Massachusetts a few years ago is set up just like you would set up a machine for the old-time Daytona Beach race. A real good soft seat helps on long runs. It's got a lot of things that work better than what they came out stock with. It's got rubber mounted handlebars, and it's got Daytona Sport Scout cams. It runs real good around sixty miles an hour. I averaged 525 miles per day. . . ."

Ownership and prospects
1920-1928 Scout
Performance and riding qualities are adequate for short rides, but patience is required

The 1938 Chief owned by Harry Sucher. The black cylinder barrels are a practical change from the original practice of nickel plating, as the nickel plating rapidly corroded. Chrome exhaust pipes became standard in 1936. *George Hays*

Riding a 1939 Sport Scout

The sit test is disappointing. The front end is tall, and the fork's long, like a modern bike. The fork rake and trail are distinctly modern, and the front end feels as heavy as a new bike when you give the bars the twist test. The full pan seat is comfy, though not as comfy as the half-pan of the 101. The compression springs of the seat work well, but not as well as the tension springs of the 101. The floorboards seem too high, and their horizontal mounting doesn't suit you as well as the slightly angled perch of the 101 floorboards. Or is your memory of the 101 getting rosier? To be sure, compared to a 101, the motor is higher off the ground, giving the Sport Scout the feel of a rigid-frame bike of the 1950s.

You need an attitude adjustment, you tell yourself. There's nothing wrong with the Sport Scout, just because it's different from a 101. Better to compare the Sport Scout to a Harley 45, you conclude.

There was a certain look that was in vogue in the 1930s, and bikes on both sides of the Atlantic took on long forks and steeply sloping top frame tubes. The Sport Scout does have dynamite looks, with its saddle tank straddling the upper frame structure. Still, with the 101 experience behind you, you understand why British old-bike enthusiasts proclaim the merits of the older, lower tank-between-the-rails motorcycles.

The motor must be the big deal, you tell yourself. You fire up the motor and it makes an angry sound despite the muffler. You blip the throttle, but the motor's a little cold natured and it stutters. You set the throttle for a fast steady idle for a minute. Now, for some more throttle twisting, and it responds eagerly. A little higher on the next blip, and still higher on the next, and on the third you let the revs soar for just an instant. The motor says let's get on with it, and you begin to get the racer feel.

You close your eyes, to see more clearly. This is the 1938 Springfield mile, and you're the world's greatest flat-tracker about to defeat the Harley gang.

Eyes open again. In gear and away. No time to spend running slow—that's not the forte of a Sport Scout. Head for a fast road and wind it up in low. It sings. Shift to second at 25 mph and more high notes. Shift to high at 50 and roar on up to 75—there's more there but you don't want to take a chance with your friend's treasure, so you back off to seventy. You look down at the engine. Yeah, it's a side-valve all right. Doesn't seem possible. Feels like a double overhead cam as it loves to rev. The exhaust resonates. One word sums up the Sport Scout—*wild.*

---

for touring, since 45 mph is about the limit for sustained running of the 37 ci Scouts. Clincher wheel rims are probably OK for riding this slowly. With one of the relatively rare pre-101 45 ci Scouts you can bump the cruising speed up to 55 mph, but at this speed clincher rims are a worry because of their habit of completely shedding the tires in a blowout or sudden flat. The antique look of the early Scout doesn't suffer much if later drop-center wheel rims are used, so you might consider this modification. A drawback to the Scout is the need to carry your own castor oil or other special oil because modern oils aren't heavy enough for total-loss lubrication.

In summary, the original Scouts aren't highly ridable, but their honorable place in motorcycling history assures the owner of keeping up with inflation. A three-star rating is the call, but selling could be a slow process since there won't be as many prospective buyers as with the later and more powerful models. Look for your total investment to be eighty to ninety percent of the cost of the reference new Harley-Davidson.

1922-1931 Chief

The ridability of these Chiefs is similar to the Scouts of the same era. Chiefs aren't as nimble and are only slightly faster cruisers than the 45 ci Scouts and 101 Scouts. Compared to the 101 Scouts, early Chiefs are real tanks.

As far as comparing early Chiefs to early Scouts, you have to decide whether you agree with the market or with longtime Indian riders and dealers. The market has for a number of years given the vote to the Chief, since a public which likes Honda Gold

In 1938, black wheel rims and cadmium spokes were standard. *George Hays*

Wings also likes big antique motorcycles. Like the early Scouts, the early Chiefs should be break-even bikes, but with a little less risk due to the higher demand than the Scouts.

Total investment for a well-restored early Chief should be eighty-five to 105 percent of the cost of the reference Harley. At press time, a Chief of this vintage carried an asking price of $12,000 or about 105 percent of our comparison Harley-Davidson.

1928-1931 Model 101 Scout

Excessive expectations can spoil an experience. For example, sometime or another, you've been disappointed in a movie that has been given the big build-up by your friends. Similarly, the 101s have a tough act to follow—their own reputation. Yet, when I took my first 101 ride, the critter completely lived up to all the rave reviews, and I was an instant convert. Could be, however, that a cultivated taste for the 101s can only be acquired after experiencing the later Indians.

In any event, owners of 101 Scouts are unanimous in their enthusiasm. Interest is keen enough to sustain a national club, The 101 Association, sometimes referred to as

Sucher's 1938 Sport Scout. The motorcycle has been fitted with the 1940 and later cylinder barrels and heads. Black finish of cylinder barrels is more practical than the original nickel-plated finish; many enthusiasts of the era used both these ideas. *George Hays*

WOW or Won-Oh-Wonders. The 101s have more fans with each passing year.

Put on drop-center rims and set up the oil pump for about 200 miles per quart, and you have a good highway runner as well as the pleasure of the famed 101 Scout handling.

I'm bucking the Chief-favoring consensus in this case, but then, any four-star rating is a vote against the consensus. As Allan Girdler said in his Illustrated Harley-Davidson Buyer's Guide, the key is to buy what most people don't want yet.

Prospects for a fully restored Scout 101 are eighty-five to 105 percent of the cost of the actual dealer's price of the Harley-Davidson FLHTC. Reasonable condition, unrestored 101s can be found for sixty to seventy percent of the reference Harley.

1932 Chief

Total-loss lubrication is the main drawback to the 1932 Chiefs. Nothing new here, but in this case the supposedly improved styling and the handling are drawbacks.

A 1938 instrument panel. This was the only year of gray instruments with red lettering, gray switch, and gray gearshift knob. *Indian 1938 dealer sales kit*

The magneto-equipped 1939 Sport Scout of Richard Ostrowski. Generator chain drive (behind clutch pedal) was unreliable. *Richard Ostrowski*

63

Back then, styling wasn't up to usual Indian standards. In today's scene, the style seems not old enough to have the full antique charm, while missing the added grace of the later Chiefs. This Chief's kind of caught in a no-man's land, you might say. Handling is heavier than the earlier Chiefs, but without the later Chief advantages of dry-sump lubrication and better styling.

Figure on paying eighty-five to 105 percent of the actual dealer's price of the Harley-Davidson FLHTC. Incidentally, the 1932 twins can be converted to dry-sump lubrication, which is recommended. Call these three-star motorcycles if dry-sump modified.

A 1939 Chief, showing the new optional World's Fair tank panel. Yet another marketing term originated at this point: from 1939 on, tuned Chief and Sport Scout motors were termed Bonneville motors, named in honor of Indian's new stock-motor records set at the Bonneville Salt Flats in 1938. Beginning in 1939, small parts like nuts and bolts were cadmium plated instead of nickel plated. *Motorcyclist*

1932-1942 Scout Pony, Junior Scout and Thirty-fifty

These motorcycles are rare—and they deserve that status, They're cute and different, and round out the collection of a few super enthusiasts who have most of everything else Indian made. Their main attractions are their easy starting, nimble handling and their unusual status at antique motorcycle shows. Total outlay should be from thirty-five to fifty percent of the comparison Harley-Davidson. The Scout Pony should run between eighty-five to 105 percent of the Harley although unrestored examples can be bought for forty to sixty percent.

1933 Motoplane

I know of only two of these in running order that have been publicized in the journal of the Antique Motorcycle Club of America. If you deal for one, it's you versus the seller, and your one deal may define the Motoplane market for the next five years.

1933-1934 Chiefs

Here, we have dry-sump lubrication fighting off ugly-duckling looks. The 1933 and 1934 Chiefs are peppier than the more coveted—and hence, more expensive—later skirted-fender models, provided you use the later-model cams and barrels on the 1933 or 1934 job. With the old-style cams and upper end, the lower power and lower weight even things out.

I think the pluses and minuses cancel out each other, and these should be break-even bikes. Plan on a total restoration investment of eighty-five to 105 percent of the actual dealer's price of the Harley-Davidson.

1934-1939 Sport Scout

Most Indian shoppers overlook the Sport Scout in favor of the Chief. They don't know what they're missing! True, the Chief has superior two-up capability, but how often do you ride double? The Chief also has a slightly higher practical cruising speed when geared tall, but the difference is indeed slight. The limit of smoothness of Chiefs is at 60-65 mph, compared to Sport Scouts at 55-60 mph. Ridden solo, the Sport Scouts will pull a little taller gearing for smoother riding over the long haul, with only a little patience required for second-gear climbing of big hills. Tall-geared Sport Scouts are right up there with Chiefs for sustained cruising. Anyway, for the extra 5 mph or less, and maybe three rides a year with a passenger, you pay thousands of dollars and steer an extra hundred-plus pounds.

Incidentally, lots of Sport Scouts were stroked to 57 ci, 935 cc by using Chief flywheels. On the open road this helps on hills, and imparts a lazier feel to the motor at speeds below 60 mph. Above 60 mph, stockers and strokers are about equally smooth.

Sport Scouts are good-looking motorcycles, even more so when parked next to the rival Harley-Davidson 45. Sport Scouts sound as if they're ready to race. While you're riding a Sport Scout, you can't help but imagine yourself as a racer of bygone days, in the middle of the Langhorne 100 flat track or the old Daytona Beach road race. When you buy a Sport Scout, you buy into all of the Indian racing mystique.

Sport Scouts are rare, but not problematically rare; just rare enough to break the monotony of Chiefs at old-bike events. The mechanical parts are fairly easy to locate, but cosmetic items may require your own effort or money to fabricate replicas. Bob Stark reports that Sport Scouts typically take about one and a half times as many hours to restore as Chiefs due to the fabrication of bits and pieces, and custom fitting of these. Somebody's probably faced any problems you might inherit with an incomplete Sport Scout, however. So club membership could pay off in the form of patterns for engine

Sport Scout with 1939 World's Fair tank panel. Tanks, however, appear to be 1935 or earlier with screw-on caps. Oversized cylinder heads are believed to be an aftermarket item. Front fender appears to be a cut-down stock fender. Handlebars, exhaust and English-style seat were factory-supplied racing accessories. The thin line protruding above the handlebars is the profile of the small windscreen, another factory accessory. Rider is Woodsie Castonguay. Locale is Daytona Beach. *Ed Kretz, Sr.*

mounting plates, footboard hardware and so on, for those who care to do their own work.

A Sport Scout racer is a good way to go. For purely show use, you can buy or fabricate some of the Indian racing accessories for extra charisma. You can keep the Scout for show, especially if the machine has a documented racing history, or make it a custom, or swap back and forth between a riding bike and a show bike.

A period custom—most emphatically *not* a chopper—is a practical, expense-cutting and authentic alternative. Lots of guys did this to new Sport Scouts, or to three- or four-year-old bikes. With a custom, not only do you end up with the authentic look of many a hot-rod bike of the era, but you get a chance to exercise a little creativity. You'll probably save some time and money by avoiding the search for rare original cosmetic items like front fenders, or the purchase of limited-production repro items.

The 45 ci Indian was the highlight of Indian engineering, and the Sport Scout carried on the Indian tradition of making new Harley-Davidson 45s a tough sell for their rivals. With a Sport Scout, I think you'll break even in the long run, and enjoy something different and classy all along the way. The three-star rating isn't my personal view—I like the Sport Scout better than the Chief—but because I know the market is dominated by Chief fans. The narrower appeal of the Sport Scout and more costly restoration also detract from the investment rating.

The first-year 1934 model should be the most coveted rigid-frame Sport Scout, so

Circa 1936 Sport Scout. Front fender, handlebars, foot pegs, exhaust and English-style saddle are factory racing accessories. Tanks have the optional Arrow-panel finish and may be over-sized racing items. Nonstandard external oil line appears to feed only the intake valve guides. Rider is Ted Edwards, Sr. Locale is Daytona Beach. *Ed Kretz, Sr.*

good bargaining is especially important on one of these rarities; the selling end will take care of itself. As an average, your total investment for a Sport Scout restored to stock configuration should be eighty-five to 105 percent of the actual dealer's price of the Harley-Davidson FLHTC. If you go the period custom route, settle for a good but nonconcours restoration and do some of your own work, your total outlay could be sixty to seventy percent of the comparison Harley cost.

1935-1939 Chief

These open-fender, rigid-frame Chiefs are rarer than the later skirted-fender jobs, but less demand results in prices about twenty percent lower than the later Chiefs. Don't look for any sleeper investment opportunities just yet, however, as the public's prefer-

ence for the later Chiefs is a long-established fact.

In my opinion, the rigid-frame Chiefs are about as comfortable as the fat-tire, spring-frame later Chiefs on today's pavement. Harley-Davidson apparently felt no threat from the spring-frame introduced on the 1940 Indians, as Harley didn't spring their big twins until 1958. But the Indian buying and selling public doesn't agree with me and Harley's management team of the 1940s; most Indian fans prefer the spring-frame. So today's rule is that although you may buy these 1933-1939 Chiefs cheaper, you'll surely sell them cheaper as well.

Still, these are solid three-star motorcycles, and they may even become four-star investments as a result of price pressure on the more popular later Chiefs. Mechanical

Circa 1940 Sport Scout racer. Special under-the-seat oil tank was built by the factory and supplied to several top riders for long events such as the Langhorne 100-mile dirt-track race and the Daytona 200-mile road race. This motorcycle was raced by Andy Dorbek. Restoration by Dick Barth.

and electrical parts are plentiful for the late 1930s Chiefs because many are the same as on later Chiefs.

Acceleration of rigid-frame Chiefs is superior to all other Indians, especially when riding double or uphill where the big pistons and relatively light weight are a happy combination.

Chiefs of this vintage offer you the chance to be really creative in selecting paint schemes, since company policy was to provide at extra charge any finish available in the DuPont inventory.

The total investment for a Chief of this vintage should be about eighty to ninety percent of the actual dealer's price of the Harley-Davidson FLHTC. In summary, these are strong three-star motorcycles, and, unlike the later Chiefs, the late 1930s Chiefs may even achieve four-star status.

Many Sport Scout flat trackers were fitted with Junior Scout tanks, such as this example ridden by Bobby Hill. Junior Scout forks were also popular for racing. Although the photo is circa 1951, the general appearance is characteristic of the 1930s and 1940s as well. Add a skinny front fender, front brake and lights, and the result would be a great-looking street cruiser. *Bobby Hill*

Chapter 3

Scouts and Chiefs 1940-1953

History
1940-1948

The skirted-fender era began in 1940, with all Indian models getting the full streamline treatment. Riders either loved or hated the new fenders; there was no in-between. The 1940 Thirty-fifty and the Sport Scout skirted-fender models were one-year-only styling entries, since both would be revamped the following year.

Rivaling the skirted fenders for attention was the new spring frame featured on the Chief and Four. The new rear suspension consisted of coil springs mounted both above and below the rear axle, the lower springs acting as recoil dampers. While travel was

The 1940 and 1941 Chiefs were nearly identical in appearance. Differences included color options, headlight, tire choices, and chrome tank strips. Optional 5.00x16 tires shown were offered beginning in 1941. *Indian archives/Bob Finn*

limited in this plunger system, the spring frame had only to compete with Harley-Davidson's unsprung rear axle.

Chief and Four tire sizes were increased from 18x4.00 to 18x4.50, with the stated purpose of accommodating the spring frame characteristics. A center stand facilitated rear tire changes on all models except the Thirty-fifty.

Unlike the skirted fenders, the newly styled Sport Scout and Chief cylinder barrels and heads were popular with everybody. Indian claimed the extra cooling fin area lowered average oil temperature by fifty degrees. An automotive-style cartridge oil filter was now standard equipment on Sport Scouts and Chiefs, and was mounted low, near the clutch pedal.

The front fork rake on all models but the Thirty-fifty was increased to provide steadier high-speed handling. Conversely, for all models a lower saddle was claimed to improve low-speed handling. A new skirted-fender sidecar rounded out the major innovations. Other changes are detailed in the captions.

Colors cataloged for 1940 were Solid Black, Seafoam (medium) Blue, and Indian Red. However, the original press releases also included Fallon Brown, Kashan Green, and Jade Green. All six colors were documented in a separately issued colors booklet. At lease one unrestored example of the Jade Green 1940 Chiefs has survived and is a consistent winner of best-unrestored trophies in the Midwest.

Several cautions concerning skirted-fender Indians are in order. Never take your banged-up skirted fenders and chainguard to the typical auto body repair shop. If you do, they'll smear Bondo all around in order to give everything a smooth finish. This works for cars, where clearances aren't critical, but doesn't work for skirted-fender Indians. Even small amounts of Bondo will prevent proper installation of the fenders and chainguard—I know, because I had to watch my expensive Chief bodywork being torched off so the job could be redone properly.

Here's something else you should know if you're gong to restore a skirted-fender Indian. Skirted rear fenders are not interchangeable from bike to bike. Back in good old Springfield, Massachusetts, workers on the final assembly line bolted the rear fender in place using four bolts, two through tabs

A 1940 Thirty-fifty. The skirted fenders were unique to this year. Larger tanks were identical to the pre-1938 Chiefs and Sport Scouts. The new front fork was a lighter version of the Sport Scout fork. *Indian 1940 dealer sales kit.*

A 1940 Sport Scout. This was the only model year to combine the rigid frame with skirted fenders, so the 1940 rear fender is unique to that year. *Indian News*

attaching the fender to the battery tray and two through tabs that connected the fender to the upper rear frame tubes. The remaining mounting holes were match-drilled to the frame. Because the four tabs were not precision parts and because the frames moved in earlier furnace brazing assembly, the exact relationship of the match-drilled holes to the tabs was unique for each fender.

Consequently, if you get your frame and fenders from different sources, you should check things out before painting the rear fender.

Year and model	1940-1945 Chief
Engine	side-valve 42 degree V-twin
Bore and stroke	3¼x4⁷/₁₆ in.
Displacement	73.62 ci
Bhp	40 (est.)
Lubrication	dry-sump
Ignition	standard, battery; optional, magneto
Gearbox	standard, three-speed; optional, four-speed or reverse; hand-actuated, sliding-gear type
Clutch	wet
Primary drive	endless four-row chain in cast-aluminum oil bath case
Wheelbase	62 in.
Wheels and tires	standard, 1940-1945, 18 in. drop-center rims, 4.50x18 tires; optional 1941-1945, 16 in. drop-center rims, 5.00x16 tires
Suspension	rear, coil compression and rebound; front, leaf-spring fork
Weight	1940-1942 skirted-fender models, 558 lb. dry; 1940-1945 open-fendered models, 538 lb. dry (est.)
Seat height	solo, 30.5 in., buddy, 33 in.
Mpg	35-45
Top speed	stock 85 mph; polished ports and precision ignition timing, 95 mph; with special cams, 100-105 mph

In 1940, Chiefs and Sport Scouts were fitted with the oil filter shown here. This proved unsuccessful because internal condensation would freeze in cold weather and stop oil flow. This was the last year of Indian script on the primary drive cover, and in fact most 1940 models had blank covers. Hurry-up catalog motorcycle had the pre–1940 small cylinder heads. *Indian 1940 catalog*

Riding a 1940 Chief

Skirted-fender Chiefs turn heads among any group of motorcyclists. During the 30,000 miles I put on my 1947 Chief, every time I rode the bike at least one person gave me a thumbs-up or a grin. Back in 1940, motorcycle fender skirts were controversial, but with the passing of years and the march of styling toward more and more enclosure, the fender skirts seem more at home today than ever before.

A ride on a 1940 Chief probably will bring three reactions. First, you'll probably love the skirted fenders.

Second, you may feel a letdown. If you've just hopped off a Chief from the mid-1930s, or if you have a good memory of that ride, you'll be disappointed at the comparative sluggishness of the 1940 Chief. The reason is simple: at 558 lb., the 1940 Chief is exactly 100 pounds heavier than the 1935 model, and fifty-four pounds heavier than the 1938 model. With the standard twenty-three-tooth transmission sprocket on the 1940 Chief, you have about the same oomph as the 1935 Chief with a twenty-five-tooth sprocket, but the latter is turning about nine percent fewer revolutions at any given speed and is consequently smoother.

Your third reaction involves the rear springs. Here, opinions vary.

What about those rear springs, you ask? You say you bet they really help? The answer is, well, sort of. The trouble with the plunger rear spring setup is that half the springs are below the axle, a simple way of providing some measure of damping in these nonhydraulic units. This means that in the some twelve inches of springing you have only an inch and a half of movement.

Care in restoration can make a big difference in the quality of the spring action. Best results are obtained by getting a set of four soft springs as used on the 1951 and 1952 Chiefs. Beyond that, you should try to get springs that are matched in stiffness and length. Putting together spring-frame plungers from a random collection of parts can result in a dragging mechanism, and in some instances the mechanism can even bind up solidly. For best results, the right and left plunger tabs that hold each end of the axle must be parallel to each other and both must be in the vertical plane—so they will keep the axle horizontal, in other words, throughout the spring movement. An improperly restored

spring-frame has scarcely any riding advantage over a rigid frame. This could have been a production problem, too, as proper functioning of plunger frames is more dependent on careful assembly than with modern swinging-arm rear suspensions.

The 1940 Chief's rear suspension works better than my 1947 Chief's. Perhaps this was because I assumed no spring-frame restoration effort was necessary; hindsight suggests I should have spent time and money checking things out. I also think the 1940 and many of the 1941-1942 spring-frame Indians had an advantage over most of the 1946-1948 Indians. The 1940 spring-frame was designed for 4.50x18 tires carrying 22 pounds per square inch (psi) pressure. When Indian later went to the popular 5.00x16 tires with only 18 psi, they didn't concurrently change the rear spring softness, which resulted in too much breakaway friction, or "stiction" as it's sometimes called.

Yes, the 1940 Chief—with 4.50x18 tires—rides smoother than a 1940 Harley-Davidson, and that's what mattered then. There were still lots of unpaved roads in 1940, and the spring-frame took some bounce out of the ride. Perhaps even more important is that the 1940 Chief gives a comfortable ride on today's highways. An odd exception is that the springs and road can produce an annoying pogo stick resonance. This is a once-in-awhile phenomenon encountered on rippled asphalt or slabbed concrete, and is usually cured by speeding up or slowing down. The sprung rear end also helps braking by keeping the rear tire on the road, whereas the rigid-frame bikes are prone to chatter under hard braking.

Another gripe is the excessive distance from the passenger seat to the passenger footrests. A passenger shorter than five feet six inches will find the leg reach uncomfortable.

Putting the Chief on its center stand is like a simple magic trick. The operation begins with the bike resting on the side stand. The rider aims the Chief straight ahead, then pulls sharply up on the right grip while pushing down on the left. The Chief will balance on the side stand with the front wheel lightly against the ground and the rear wheel aloft. The rider either reaches down to move the center stand down manually, or optionally flicks the center stand down with his foot. With the center stand down, the rider completes the magic by simply letting the Chief come back to the vertical position, and the bike climbs up onto the center stand. Besides being a practical feature, this is a fun trick to pull right beside some couple who've just groaned and grunted and barely been able to get their Gold Wing or Harley onto the center stand!

To sum up a 1940 Chief ride, you can call it pleasant. The skirted fenders make this more of a crowd pleaser than the earlier jobs and you'll draw attention on every ride. The power, smoothness and ride are more than adequate for modern freeway speeds.

1940-1944 Military development

The American defense build-up began in the late 1930s, so even before Pearl Harbor both Indian and Harley-Davidson were emphasizing military planning. The Allied Powers, being nations that had emphasized the development of 500 cc motorcycles, included this capacity in their military specifications for solo motorcycles. This, and the receptiveness of the American military to

Allied thinking in general, for a time resulted in a bias toward this capacity in the motorcycle plans of the US Army.

With an eye to foreign military sales as well as to the US government, Indian bet their military chips on a 30.50 ci, 500 cc version of the Sport Scout called the Model 741. Despite the model designation 741, initial production and critical competitive testing were carried out in 1939. The Army's pref-

Although shown hitched to a postwar Chief, this sidecar design became available in 1940. *George Hays*

A 1940 45 ci, 750 cc Dispatch Tow. *Indian dealer sales kit*

The Indian Chief was favored by many police departments, and naturally by the Springfield, Massachusetts, police as shown here. Samples of state police organizations using the Chief (numbers of Chiefs in parentheses) were Pennsylvania (602), Massachusetts (237), North Carolina (103), Texas (80) and Maryland (45). Some cities using Chiefs were New York City (480), Philadelphia (126, includes some Scouts) and Boston (100). Nationwide, 70 percent of the population was policed on Indians. *Indian archives/Bob Finn*

erence for the Harley-Davidson 45 was made official in early 1940, and Indian missed out on large US orders. Meanwhile, the 741 designation stuck, probably because the first substantial Indian military contracts carried over from 1940 to 1941.

For breathing, the 741 had the Thirty-fifty style of T manifold instead of the Sport Scout Y manifold. Ground clearance was increased by longer forks and by rear frame alteration, and an automotive-style oil bath air cleaner was added.

Although few 741s were used by US forces, substantial numbers of the Indian 741 were sold to the Allies. As a result, fair numbers of 741s can be found today in Britain, Europe, Australia and New Zealand— probably more than can be found in the United States. Many 45 ci versions of the mid-size Indian military twin (with Y-manifold) were sold to Canadian forces as the Model 640–B, all with sidecars.

While Harley-Davidson got the bulk of American military motorcycle business, Indian built a lot of Chiefs for the French government in the earliest phase of World War Two, and later, for other American allies. These Chiefs were essentially built to

1940 civilian specifications except that there were no fender skirts, no chrome, and paint was to military specifications, mostly olive drab.

During 1941, Indian and Harley-Davidson developed shaft-drive military motorcycles, each hoping to win large production contracts. Harley's Model XA was a copy of the German BMW, but Indian's was a new design from wheels to wheel. Only 1,000 of this Model 841 were built, the same as the rival Harley-Davidson XA, and few saw any military duty other than testing. The US military had discovered the Jeep, and needed no more motorcycles to augment their standard Harley 45s.

The 841 development had postwar civilian carryovers. The 841 rubber-mounted handlebars and a narrower and longer version of the 841 fork were used on the 1946-1948 Chiefs. Additionally, the 841 wheel hubs and brakes were destined for postwar Chiefs.

Another project was the model M1 lightweight single-cylinder side-valve motorcycle of 13.5 ci, 221cc displacement. The M1 girder forks looked like scaled-down 841 forks. The right-side primary drive case appeared to be the same design used on the postwar vertical twin and single. This is more than a coincidence. Fred Crismon says

Bobber styling was the common treatment given to older Indians during the 1930s and 1940s—the racy looks cost less than replacing original cosmetics. Also, many a new Indian was done up in the Bobber style and new front fenders were hauled to the dumps in truckloads! This 1935 Chief Bobber is fitted with 1939 crankcases and 1940 or later cylinders and heads. Restoration by Gene Grimes.

in his book *US Military Wheeled Vehicles* that the M1 was termed the Model 148 by Indian, who termed their similar-sized 1949 Arrow the Model 149.

The 241 lb., 6.2 bhp M1 was designed for paratroops and was declared operational in December 1944. From the scant publicity the M1 has received, however, it seems likely that the project never went beyond the prototype stage. Unsubstantiated rumor says that at least one of the M1s finished its career at the Army depot in Waterloo, New York.

1941-1945 civilian production

The headliner of the 1941 catalog was the new spring-frame Sport Scout. Comfort and appearance were improved with this smaller version of the Chief and Four coil-spring setup. But, the Sport Scout spring-frame brought a weight penalty that added to the gradual weight growth of its rigid-frame predecessor. The 1941 Sport Scout's cataloged weight of 500 lb. was just four pounds lighter than the 1938 Chief's! The Sport

Scout had added 115 pounds since its 1934 origin. Performance had accordingly diminished over the years, and in the opinion of some, had become unacceptable in the 1941 models.

The 1941 Thirty-fifty shed its fender skirts and got a more up-to-date front fender. Indian's little twin also reverted to the old crotch-style gearshift. Only one finish was available on the Thirty-fifty: a black frame and forks with red tanks and fenders.

The following changes were incorporated on all models but the Thirty-fifty. A chrome-plated sealed-beam headlight replaced the earlier black unit with bulb. Single-color finishes were black, blue and red, but five optional two-color finishes were now offered as well. These consisted of red and white, blue and white, black and white, black and red, and black and blue. In each combination, the first color mentioned was used on the tops of the fenders and the tanks, while the second color was used on the fender skirts, chainguard and toolbox. Not many 1941

The 1940 and 1941 Sport Scout barrels and heads were welcomed by Bobber fans. The 101 shown here belongs to Helen Henderson Clifford, descendant of the motorcycling Hendersons.

Indians have been restored in the two-color schemes, so here's your chance to do something different, although most find it gaudy. Although not a cataloged option, occasional photos of solid white Indian Chiefs and Fours appeared in *Indian News,* the company's house organ, so the completely white finish was probably built up in advance of orders.

The 1941 Chiefs and Sport Scouts got a new oil pump; this was becoming a traditional new feature every few years, and you wonder why they couldn't get it right to begin with. Oh well, Harley-Davidson was playing the same game. Anyway, the new pump had a claimed fifty-seven percent increase in oil circulation. Another lubrication change was the elimination of the external oil filter. The filter was unattractive, but more importantly was unsuitable for winter riding because of the tendency to collect condensation which would freeze.

A design change resulted in lighter pistons for all models. The standard solo seat got an inch and a half of foam rubber padding instead of a half-inch of horsehair.

I swim against the flow on the next alleged improvement, the optional provision of 5.00x16 tires in lieu of 4.50x18 tires. Indian also got tired of swimming upstream on this issue, and after publishing articles decrying the use of 5.00x16 tires, finally gave up and offered them. Harley-Davidson was the first to offer these tires because a rigid-frame Harley with 5.00x16 tires was about as comfortable as a spring-frame Indian with 4.50x18 tires. In the 1940s and 1950s both Harley and Indian riders preferred the 5.00x16 tires, some just for the substantial look of the big tires. Not me. Even as a kid I thought one reason British bikes looked so good was that they didn't have "car" tires like Harleys and Indians.

Almost everybody still prefers these fat tires. My main objection to 5.00x16 tires is that they rob the motorcycle of agility and handling sensitivity. They're comfortable, however, and my 30,000 miles of Chief riding were aboard 5.00x16 tires. I kept them because I was too cheap to buy new wheels and tires, and because 5.00x16 tires gave my 1947 Chief the authentic look.

Limited rear spring travel is indicated. Half of the impressive rear springing is below the axle, to act as rebound damping. Stiff springing was softened during the War, in 1946 and 1952.

Because Indian was busy with military orders, very few 1942 civilian Indians were produced and no 1942 catalog was issued. No civilian Thirty-fifty models were produced. From photos appearing in *Indian News,* the only cosmetic change to the few 1942 civilian Chiefs was a new tank badge with an

The long reach for the passenger's legs is shown in this photo. This passenger is five feet nine inches tall.

Some idea of the easy center stand operation is indicated here. A ninety-pound weakling can do the job.

Indian head in profile. Some Sport Scouts were assembled with open fenders and rigid frames. The factory wasn't able to continue stocking accessories due to metal shortages. When chrome trim items were depleted from inventory, they were replaced with enameled parts. All of the standard 1941 colors were available on 1942 Indians, except

Year and model	1940-1941 Sport Scout
Engine	side-valve 42 degree V-twin
Bore and stroke	stock, 2⅞x3½ in.; with turned-down Chief flywheels, 2⅞x4⁷⁄₁₆ in.
Displacement	stock, 45.44 ci, 744.6 cc; stroked, 57.6 ci, 943.9 cc
Bhp	stock, 25 (est.); tuned, 35-38 (est.); stroked, 30 (est.)
Lubrication	dry-sump
Ignition	standard, battery; optional, magneto
Gearbox	standard, three-speed; optional four-speed or reverse; hand-actuated, sliding-gear
Clutch	wet
Primary drive	endless three-row chain in cast-aluminum oil bath case
Wheelbase	58 in.
Wheels and tires	standard, 1940–1941, 18 in. drop-center rims, 4.00x18 tires; optional 1941, 16 in. drop-center rims, 5.00x16 tires
Suspension	rear, coil compression and rebound; front, girder
Weight	1940, 475 lb.; 1941, 500 lb.
Seat height	solo, 30 in., buddy, 32 in.
Mpg	55 (advertised)
Top speed	stock, 85 mph; polished ports and precision ignition timing, 95 mph; with special cams, 100-105 mph; stroked, 95 mph

for Police Silver which was replaced by Police Gray.

A few civilian Chiefs with open fenders were built during the war, and made avail-

A 1941 Sport Scout. Chrome tank strips were added to the 1941 models (except the thirty-

fifty) after the catalog was published. *Indian archives/Bob Finn*

A 1941 Thirty-fifty. Open fenders returned to the little twin. The front fender is another one-year-only item, unless a few 1942s were made. Note that old-style clincher rims were used throughout the little twin's production. *Indian archives/ Bob Finn*

Model 741 military motorcycle. This was a small-bored and destroked version of the Sports Scout, but with a T manifold like the Junior Scout. Sport Scout front fork and upper rear frame tubes were lengthened to increase ground clearance; the 1948 racers also used these parts. *Indian archives/Ian Campbell*

able for police sales or for essential civilian transportation, the latter requiring the cutting of much red tape prior to government approval for each sale. During this period, the rear springing was slightly softened to combat stiction.

1946-1951

After the war, the Indian line consisted of the Chief only. DuPont became interested in selling off Indian, so there was no advantage in taking additional risks continuing any but the most popular of Indian models. In 1946, a much softer front suspension was achieved on the Chief, with a new girder fork similar to the one used on the experimental military Model 841 shaft-drive. Front axle travel was increased from about two inches to about five inches. Speaking from 30,000 miles of experience I can vouch for the comfort of the Indian girder fork. In fact, I consider this fork more comfortable than modern telescopics around town at less than 40 mph, and the reason is the total lack of stiction.

Again, the rear springing was softened. The Indian-head tank emblems of the wartime civilian models were continued on the 1946 Chiefs.

For 1947, the Indian-head emblems were replaced by Indian script. The front fender light was changed to the Indian-head design. The chainguard was trimmed down, so that the kickstarter crank was no longer completely encircled by sheet metal. A foul up with the ammeter supplier, or perhaps just carelessness at the Indian factory, resulted in a unique ammeter for late-1946 and all 1947 models. The new ammeter was rotated in its mounting, so that the neutral needle position (no charge or discharge) was angled forty-five degrees to the right, rather than being vertical.

The 1947 self-aligning clutch release bearings were proclaimed as an improvement; however, these bearings didn't work out and the old style was reinstated until the end of production in 1953. Prior to 1948, the rear exhaust header, muffler and tailpipe were

Model 841 military motorcycle. A unique Indian design, this motorcycle was powered by a 45 ci, 750 cc transverse V-twin with mostly Sport

Scout internals. This was Indian's first foot-shift machine. *Indian archives/George Hays*

built as a single unit which was attached to the front header by a clamp located near the right floorboard. Beginning in 1948, the front and rear exhaust headers were built as a single unit which was joined to the one-piece muffler and tailpipe by a clamp located near the kickstarter.

During 1947, Indian dealers sold Czechoslovakian CZ 125 cc motorcycles. These handshift lightweights were not branded as Indians.

The instrument panel that had been used since 1938 was redesigned for 1948, and the ammeter was replaced by a generator warning light. The speedometer was changed from the Corbin unit to a fancier Stewart-Warner unit with the needle shaped like an Indian arrow. The speedometer was now driven from the front wheel.

In mid-1948, Chief front fork shackle bearings were changed from needle bearings to bushings, and grease fittings were added. On the Chief frame, the upper crossbrace behind the seat post was changed from a straight tube to a rectangular cross-sectioned

A 1944 Chief. A few of these open-fender spring-framed Chiefs were made available to civilians for transportation connected with defense industry jobs. Military Chiefs looked much the same except for the olive drab color and lack of the Indian-head tank badge. The Indian-head tank badge appeared earlier on the last few Indians built as 1942 models, and later, on the 1946 Chiefs. *Hill/Bentley*

The Model 841. The fork design was later lengthened and narrowed for use on the postwar Chiefs. *Indian archives/George Hays.*

piece formed into an arc following the rear fender's curve.

For the 1948 season, Indian built the last of the Sport Scouts, the Model 648 Daytona Scout. By now, the firm had been sold by DuPont to the Ralph Rogers group and almost all company effort was focused on development of a new line of lightweight vertical twins and singles. Consequently, only fifty Model 648s were assembled, plus an undetermined stock of spare parts.

The 648 included a number of new internal features. The flywheels were narrower and were made of cast steel instead of iron. Oil passages in the crankshaft assembly were graduated instead of uniform size. The front camshaft was altered to drive the new 1948 Chief aluminum oil pump. The pistons

A 1947 Chief. A front-to-rear tour reveals the following parts which are available as reproduction items: front fender tip, front fender trim, Indian-head fender light, front fender, headlight, windshield mounting bar, rubber-mounted handlebar mounts, handlebars, brake lever, handgrips, tank-top instrument panel, oil and gas caps, Indian script on gas tank, exhaust headers, buddy seat, buddy seat rail, buddy seat spring mechanism, distributor cap, wiring harness tube, floorboards, passenger floorboard extensions, kickstarter pedal, chainguard, muffler and tailpipe, rear fender, rear spring covers, rear fender trim, luggage rack, taillight, stoplight, rear fender brace, and rear fender bumper. In short, just about everything is available for postwar Chiefs. *Sam Hotton*

were more domed than earlier Sport Scouts', which required reshaping of the combustion chambers.

The 648 external appearance was also altered. Most noticeable was a large built-in sump cast in the rear of the cases. This gave the model the nickname "big base." The oil pump drove a vertically mounted magneto, and the tight fit required the cutting away of several cylinder cooling fins.

Most of the big-base Scout development was done in the 1940 and 1941 racing seasons, when several prototypes were made available under the table to favored riders. Such a covert big-base Scout won the 1947 Daytona 200, and a Model 648 repeated the feat in the 1948 Daytona 200.

In 1948 the CZ 125 cc bikes, now with footshift, continued to be sold from Indian dealerships. An Indian decal was now affixed above the CZ logo on the gas tank. The CZ continued to be offered in 1949.

Indian neither cataloged nor built in quantity any 1949 Chiefs because of the move to a new one-story factory and the organization of the assembly line for the new vertical twins and singles. Some fifty to one hundred Chiefs were assembled in 1949 with telescopic forks, footshift and hand clutch, but these were designated 1950 models.

The two biggest changes for 1950 were the enlargement of the Chief from 74 ci, 1200 cc to 80 ci, 1300 cc, and the official arrival of telescopic forks. The displacement increase was achieved through the simple expedient of increasing the stroke from $4\frac{7}{16}$ to $4\frac{13}{16}$ in. The 1950 and 1951 Chiefs were identically styled, featuring slightly smaller front fenders than the earlier jobs. Also in 1950, for the first time the right-hand throttle and left-hand shift were standard, ending a forty-nine-year Indian tradition of left-hand throttles. Many Indians had been converted to right-hand throttles over the years, however.

For full-dress bikes, a problem of Indian skirted-fender styling is revealed in the photo here. The dramatic lines of the skirted rear fenders are obscured by the addition of saddlebags, the machine as a whole appearing half streamlined and half Harley. More-

Year and model	1946-1948 Chief
Engine	side-valve 42 degree V-twin
Bore and stroke	$3\frac{1}{4}$x$4\frac{7}{16}$ in.
Displacement	73.62 ci
Bhp	40 (est.)
Lubrication	dry-sump
Ignition	standard, battery; optional, magneto
Gearbox	standard, three-speed; optional four-speed or reverse; hand-actuated, sliding-gear
Clutch	wet
Primary drive	endless four-row chain in cast-aluminum oil bath case
Wheelbase	1946, 61 in.; 1947-1948, 60 in.
Wheels and tires	1946 standard, 4.50x18; optional, 5.00x16; 1947-1948 standard, 5.00x16; optional 4.50x18
Suspension	rear, coil compression and rebound; front, girder fork
Weight	550 lb.
Seat height	solo, 29.5 in., buddy, 31.5 in.
Mpg	35-45
Top speed	stock, 85 mph; polished ports and precision ignition timing, 95 mph; with special cams, 100-105 mph

over, the high-style exhaust restricted the size of saddlebags that could be mounted above the pipes, and even so, Chief riders

Model 648 Daytona Sport Scout. Fifty of these special racers were assembled by a three-man crew in the experimental department. Longer Model 741 forks and upper rear frame tubes were used. Cylinders were the Model 841 design. *Indian archives/Jimmy Hill and Matt Keevers*

Riding a 1951 Chief

The appeal of the higher-compression long-stroke 80 ci, especially at about 55 mph, can't be denied, and the power impulses seem particularly unburdened. The transmission sprocket was standardized at twenty-five teeth, and the extra cubic inches and sportier cams compensate for the taller gearing and the weight growth since the mid-thirties.

Another advantage of the 80s is the notable increase in acceleration from a standing start. A quarter-mile can be turned in about fifteen seconds, and while this may sound like a joke compared to modern bikes, considerable time in a quarter-mile digout is lost shifting to second, and considerable rpm are lost with the shift. Out on the highway, the kind of power an 80 Chief puts out is deceiving, feeling more like 100 hp than forty or fifty. The power is there for the asking, at the twist of the grip.

On the minus side, I don't care for the tall front end of the telescopic Chiefs when equipped with 5.00x16 tires. This goes double for Chiefs with the traditional sprung buddy seat—and most of them are so-equipped. The problem is, Indian didn't make any frame changes when they brought in the telescopics. Thus, the longer telescopics simply jack up the front end by the amount of the extra fork length, about two and a half inches when the telescopic forks are unloaded. Squeezing the front brake lever and pushing the motorcycle forward compresses the fork springs, perhaps a little more than average riding conditions, until a telescopic Chief is one inch taller than a girder Chief. If you're less than six feet tall, there's no longer the good feeling of planting your feet flat on the ground at a stoplight. This seems so un-Indian. The feel is (ugh!) modern, like so many contemporary cruisers that have their wheels too far out front to handle lightly.

could stuff these bags so heavily that the attendant sag resulted in a burned-out right saddlebag. Burned saddlebags are less likely if the bags are mounted to the fender crown as was the common practice in the 1940s and 1950s, but most restorers prefer mounting them to the fender skirts—and thus the problem is more prevalent today.

Model 648. Floorboards had not yet been installed. Completed 648s were ridden down the hallway, then over a bridge covered with corrugated tin, into another factory building for dynamometer testing. The noise in the tin-covered bridge was deafening, recalled leader Jimmy Hill. *Indian archives/Jimmy Hill and Matt Keevers*

and tailpipe peculiar to the 1940 models could be problems you will have to solve by fabrication. Mechanical and electrical parts are relatively easy to locate, although sometimes more expensive than the more common Chief parts. Restoration cost is usually higher for a Sport Scout than for a Chief because of additional labor required to fabricate floorboard-mounting hardware and exhaust systems. The thirty-five pounds of weight growth over the 1939 model may not be noticeable, but the 1939 Sport Scout was already fifty-five pounds heavier than the inaugural 1934 model, so the total weight climb from 1934 through 1940 is 90 pounds.

I've seen five skirted-fender 1941 Sport Scouts in California during the past ten years, and several have been featured in the journal of the Antique Motorcycle Club of America. This indicates a higher survival rate for the 1941s than for the 1940s, and probably means sellers will demand a premium for this long-recognized classic. Therefore, I believe the investment value is no better than for the earlier Sport Scouts.

The rear fender, muffler and tailpipe peculiar to the 1941 models may prove costly fabrication projects. A stock 1941 Sport Scout weighs 500 lb., about the same as a 1939 Chief, so performance is below the Sport Scout reputation set by the earlier rigid-frame models. Personally, I think the 1941 Sport Scout is the most attractive of the spring-frame Indians. When stroked to 57 ci, the 1941 Sport Scout will have about the same acceleration as a 45 ci rigid-frame model.

I'm not happy to rate the Sport Scouts as average investments, because they're high on my personal list of favorites. The market for the 1930s and 1940s is dominated by Chiefs, however. The American love of big

Rainbow Chief, a custom style developed by John Polovik in 1942. Bob Stark designed the foot shift mechanism. Hand-clutch actuation uses Harley-Davidson parts. Restoration by Bob Stark.

A 94 ci, 1542 cc Chief bobber with rainbow tank. Engine dimensions achieved with 3⅛ in. bore and 5½ in. stroke—and minimal piston skirts!

Front fender and ornament were used on 1956-1959 Royal Enfield Indians. Harley-Davidson taillight. Restoration by Bob Stark.

motorcycles has never been more evident than in the 1980s, so there's every reason to believe that Sport Scouts will continue to be riskier investments than Chiefs.

1948 Daytona Sport Scout

A couple of points must be stressed: first, there's real history here; second, everybody has recognized this for years. The biggest drawback to the Model 648 is that it appeals to an even smaller group than Sport Scouts in general. If you buy a 1948 Sport Scout racer, investment should be viewed as a long-haul matter. A planned methodical selling campaign should bring the all-important break-even return in terms of real dollars,

but a hurried sale is likely to bring less satisfactory results than with a Chief.

1950-1952 Chief

The footshift 1950 and the handshift 1950-1952 telescopic models are just as functional as the much coveted 1953s. In relation to dollars spent versus value received, all of the telescopic Chiefs suffer from price pressure. In my judgment, the premium asked for most of these telescopic Chiefs is not worth the difference compared to the 1940-1948 models. The telescopic Chiefs are just as safe a way to park your money as the earlier skirted-fender Chiefs, but the higher parking fee isn't going to give you a bigger percentage of appreciation. If you ride a lot, you'll probably break even; if you seldom ride, you'll make a little.

Prices of the 1950-1952 telescopic Chiefs, when professionally restored, should be in the neighborhood of 100-150 percent of the actual dealer's price of the Harley-Davidson FLHTC. In 1989, the author underestimated the price escalation of these models.

1953 Chiefs

Many collectors prefer the last of the breed, the 1953 Chiefs, or at least they prefer the 1953 Chiefs until they learn about the price premium asked for the 1953s.

An interesting point is that Indian made almost the same number of 1952 and 1953 Chiefs, about 700 in 1952 and 600 in 1953, yet club rosters invariably list more 1953s than 1952s. Sometimes, this dates back to the original sale, when the initial rush of collecting interest in late 1953 motivated buyers to grab

1952 Chiefs that had been gathering dust in showrooms. Dealers simply documented these 1952 leftovers as 1953s, and in some states this was the law then in effect. In other cases, restorers have managed to get their former basket cases registered as 1953s, when the motorcycles may have been anything from 1948 or later.

I may catch some flak on this, because there's no denying that 1953 Chiefs have drawing power, but in my opinion there's seldom a way of being assured the 1953 you're looking at is really a 1953. A professional restorer strongly disagrees with me on this point, stating emphatically that he can tell the real thing from a phony. Well, my comeback is that everybody who buys doesn't have his expertise. Hence, unless you have some kind of unusual and irrefutable proof of authenticity, there's no sense paying a premium for a 1953 Chief as compared to the other telescopic fork jobs, the

Typical full dress late Chief. This is a 1948 model fitted with 1952-1953 cosmetics except for the 1948 chainguard and exhaust system. The threat of burned saddlebags is apparent. The luggage box is the metal Scoot Boot sold in the fifties for attachment to outboard motors—a real status symbol now. Restoration by Bob Stark.

1950-1952 models. Even if you know yours really is a 1953, is it worth extra thousands?

Another debate with the professional restorer followed, and the talk merits mention because this takes us right back to the ideas of standards expressed in the opening pages. Given that 1953 Chiefs generally bring higher prices than 1952 Chiefs, it doesn't necessarily follow that 1953 Chiefs are better investments than 1952 Chiefs. If today the 1953 is worth X percent more than the 1952, and if ten years hence the 1953 is

worth the same X percent more, the investment contest is a tie.

As investments, the 1953 Chiefs are as safe as the earlier Chiefs, but they aren't likely to make you any more in terms of percentage and they tie up a lot of money. If you can get a 1953 without paying more than a ten-percent premium for its last-year status, this is another three-star machine. If you shell out more than ten percent extra for last-year status, you've got yourself a somewhat riskier two-and-a-half-star in-

The last Indians? According to the late Walt Brown, then production supervisor, this photo shows the assembly of the last American-built Indians during May 1953. Brown is standing near the middle of the photo, with sleeves rolled up. The motorcycles are being prepared for the New York City police. Brown also said that the last civilian Chiefs were assembled in February

1953. Brown added that the activity with the civilian Chief in the foreground was purely for photo purposes, to give the false impression that civilian Chiefs were still in production. Over the years, a story has circulated that another batch of 50 police Chiefs and five extra civilian Chiefs were built as 1955 models. Brown wasn't at Indian when that might have happened.

vestment, and later on you'll have to do the same super sales job on your buyer in order to come out even.

If you're hot for a last-of-the-line 1953 Chief, despite my earlier caution, the upper limit for a perfect professionally restored Chief can exceed 175 percent of the current Harley-Davidson actual dealer's price FLHTC. In 1989, the author underestimated the price escalation of these models.

A final note on the final Chiefs. Contrary to rumors, there were probably no 1955 Chiefs. This claim was refuted in 1987 in the Antique Motorcycle Club of America magazine by Emmett Moore and Walt Brown, ex-Indian employees. Brown said that he built the last Chief in 1953. Brown was not at Indian when the fabled batch of fifty-five 1955s was supposedly assembled. Bob Finn was still in the sales half of the split company; he does not recall any 1955 Chiefs.

Bobbers and customs.

These are break-even bikes; however, this category does not include choppers that have had major alterations done to the frame and forks. In the eyes of antique motorcycle enthusiasts, a nonstock rake is simply a major job that will have to be undone to make the Chief acceptable. Chop a Chief and you cut its value. Expect the buyer interest in period bobbers to be generally less than for stock Chiefs. Prices for bobbers and period customs are extremely varied, some being shortcut bikes, others representing considerable innovation by their builders.

Rainbows, however, draw as much interest as stockers. For a professionally executed rainbow paint job, which requires several layers of paint, you should reserve about double the cost of a standard professional paint job.

Skirted-fender encore. Stock 1953 Chief. *Indian archives/Bob Finn.*

Chapter 4

Not ratable	1927-1928 Indian Ace and 1929 Model 401
★★★┛	1929-1931 Model 402
★★★	1932-1933 Model 403 and 1934 Model 434
★★★┛	1935 Model 435
★★┛	1936-1937 Model 436 and 437
★★★	1938-1942 Model 438-442
Not ratable	1947 Torque Four

Indian Fours: Duesenbergs of motorcycling 1927-1942

History
1927-1935

There were four prominent four-cylinder American motorcycles in the early part of the century: the Pierce, the Cleveland, the Henderson and the Ace. The Pierce was a copy of the Belgian FN, and was made from 1909 through 1913 by a company better known for the Pierce Arrow automobile. The Cleveland was built from 1925 through

1929 by a family whose main income was derived from manufacturing screws and other hardware. The Henderson was designed by Will Henderson, whose firm was run by himself and brother Tom from 1912 until 1917, when the brothers then sold out to Ignatz Schwinn—yes, the bicycle guy.

The Henderson brothers worked in Schwinn's Excelsior-Henderson organization for a couple of years, and then left to design

The original Indian Four was simply an Ace Four with the Indian decal, red paint and smaller wheels. The Ace frame had a single front down-tube. The next generation of Fours was the Model 401 with Ace frame and leaf-spring fork. *Indian 1928 catalog*

and produce another motorcycle, the Ace. The Ace was produced under the management of the Henderson brothers from 1920 through 1922, when Will was killed in a motorcycle accident. Afterward, the Ace changed hands twice in the mid-twenties.

In 1927, the Indian company purchased the Ace rights and tooling, and by the following spring Indian was manufacturing the Indian Ace. The Indian Ace differed from the original Ace only in the use of Indian Red paint, the Indian logo with small Ace subscript and the use of smaller wheels.

The Indian Ace of 1927 and 1928 gave way to the Indian Four Model 401 of 1929. The principal changes were the characteristic Indian leaf spring fork in lieu of the Ace leading link, Harley-style fork, the addition of a front brake, and a more streamlined tank in common with the 101 Scout. The cataloged weight grew from 395 to 455 lb.

Toward the end of the Model 401 production run in April 1929, a new double down-tube frame was used in lieu of the Ace single down-tube frame. This change was made to reduce vibration. Not officially cataloged, these hybrids of a three-main-bearing engine and later-model frame were registered as regular Model 401s.

The Model 401 was officially replaced by the Model 402 in May 1929. In the 402, the Ace three-main-bearing crankshaft was replaced by a new five-main-bearing shaft. Additionally, the change to a double down-

The small size of the pre-1932 Indian Fours is apparent in this photo of Max Bubeck with his 1930 Four. Black wheel rims are correct. Handlebars are bent to rider's preference, as in the good old days.

Intake rocker arms are a Bubeck design featuring needle roller bearings. The white area at the base of the front intake pushrod is a modern neoprene cup seal installed to keep oil in and dirt out; other intake seals are obscured by the exhaust manifold. The seals work well on 1928-1935 Fours, which have round cross-section lifters. The 1936-1937 Fours have oblong cross-section lifters, and seals won't work.

Oil cooler and filter shown here. These beautiful crankcases are in short supply.

tube frame was made official by way of company advertising and service literature. In 1931, the old external contracting band rear brake was replaced with an internal expanding brake, otherwise the late 1929 through 1931 Fours were identical.

All Aces, Indian Aces and Indian Fours from 1920 through 1937 featured exposed pushrods. Unfortunately, the standard pushrod arrangement resulted in dirt being ingested into the engine, where it formed a lapping compound and greatly accelerated wear, plugged up oil passages, and insured oil seepage onto the exterior of the engine. Modern auto intake-valve lifter neoprene cup seals can be installed, an important cure which keeps the dirt out and the oil in, and doesn't detract from the period appearance. On 1928 through 1935 Fours this modification can be used with the round valve lifters. The 1936 and 1937 Fours had oblong cross-section lifters, so the seals won't work.

In 1932, the Four received a new taller frame with longer front forks. Functionally, the new layout was progress in reverse. Weight had now climbed to 500 lb., a ten percent climb without any additional power to compensate. Even without the extra weight, the higher front end probably would've taken some of the life out of the handling.

The 1932 configuration continued for 1933 and 1934. In the latter year, DuPont got carried away and offered twenty-four standard color options, including a variety of two-color finishes. Just in case you didn't see what you wanted with these twenty-four standard options, for $5 extra you could specify any color available in DuPont Duco Lacquer!

New styling was given to the Four in 1935. The 1935 model is unusual in that this was the last year of the Ace engine layout and the first year of the new styling.

1936-1942

A turning point in the Indian versus Harley-Davidson rivalry came in 1936. Harley brought out their successful overhead-valve V-twin, the 61 OHV, and Indian introduced their unsuccessful "upside-down" Four, the Model 436. The upside-down label came from the reversal of the valve configuration, the intake valves were now housed on the side and the exhaust valves moved upstairs. The idea was to increase power, although it's doubtful whether any significant improvement resulted.

The clear result was a more cluttered look and the "upside-down" nickname, an unfortunate inference that Indian engineering was confused. Another detriment was the greater likelihood of overheating the rider's right leg, especially if any exhaust leaks were present. The late Sam Pierce, known as "Mr. Indian," who used to restore Steve McQueen's Redskins, was known for thinking with his heart when the subject was Indian motorcycles. But even the upside-down Fours were too much for Pierce, who once said that the 1936 Indian Four was the worst motorcycle ever built. The upside-down plumbing was continued in 1937, with the exception of changing to twin carburetors.

Four-lovers rejoiced in 1938, when the engine was completely redesigned and the normal valve configuration was returned to the F-head layout with overhead intake and side exhaust valves. The cylinders were cast in pairs, which gave a much more attractive appearance. Other major changes included complete valve gear enclosure and automatic valve lubrication. The result was a considerable improvement, and the entire motorcycle was classic. Yet hindsight tells us that in either 1936 or 1938 Indian would have been wiser to have canceled the Four and spent the engineering time and money on a new overhead-valve twin to go head to head with the Harley-Davidson 61 OHV.

The cluttered left side of a Four was seldom shown in company advertisements. Note clutch pedals, plural. The rider could move his or her foot to the right and push the small sub-pedal down with the main pedal, in order to lock the clutch disengaged while stopped. On the upstroke, a dab on the main pedal released the lockout. The Crocker steering damper was made by the same company that built the Crocker V-twins.

Year and model . . . . 1928-1942 Four
Engine . . . . Inline four-cylinder
1928-1935: overhead inlet valves, side exhaust valves
1936-1937: side inlet valves, overhead exhaust valves
1938-1942: overhead inlet valves, side exhaust valves
Bore and stroke . . . . 2¾x3¼ in.
Displacement . . . . 77.21 ci, 1265 cc
Bhp . . . . 1928-1935: 30 (est.)
   1936-1937: 35 (est.)
   1938-1942: 40 (est.) With special tuning, 50 (est.)
Gearbox . . . . three-speed, hand-shift, sliding-gear
   engagement for 2nd, dog engagement for 1st and 3rd.
Wheelbase . . . . 1928-1931: 59½ in.
   1932-1939: 61 in.
   1940-1942: 62 in.
Wheels . . . . 1928-1942: 18 in. (early catalog references
   were 25 or 26 in. but included tire diameter) 16 in. optional
   for 1940-1942
Tires . . . . 1928: 18x3.85 (catalog called this 25x3.85)
1929-1939: 4.00x18 (early catalog refers to 26x4.00)
1940-1942: 4.50x18 standard; 1941-1942, 5.00x16 optional.
Suspension . . . . . . 1928-1939: front, leaf spring; rear, rigid
1940-1942: front, leaf spring; rear, coil springs in plunger
Weight . . . . 1928: 385 lb.
   1929-1931: 455 lb.
   1932-1937: 515 lb.
   1938-1939: 532 lb.
   1940-1942: 568 lb.
Mpg . . . . 50 (est.)
Top speed . . . . 1928-1935: 75 mph (est.)
1936-1937: 80 mph (est.)
1938-1942: stock, 90 mph (est.); with heavy valve springs,
   polished ports and larger carburetor, 108.43 mph electrically timed, rider Max Bubeck

For 1939, the Four was changed only cosmetically.

In recent years, a few Fours have been spotted with 1938 style engines in 1936-1937 style frames. Some of these hybrids may have originated in mid-1937, near the end of the production run of 1937 models. Indian often made running changes, so it would have been in character for them to have used up all stocks of 1936-1937 style frames after the 1938 motors were available. In California, two of the hybrids carry 1937 numbers on both the frame and engine. On the other hand, the two "1937½" Fours may have been factory-modified later with the 1938 style engine. The Indian factory upgraded at least two 1936 Fours to the 1938 engine specifications, leaving the engine numbers as 1936 numbers. These two Fours were advertised to dealers through the company dealer publication *Service Shots* for December 5, 1938.

The year 1940 ushered in the last general type, the skirted-fender series. Weight now had climbed to 568 lb., thirty-six pounds more than the rigid-frame 1939.

Indian gave in to the fad for fat tires and made 5.00x16 tires optional on the 1941 Four. Most skirted-fender Fours have been fitted with these tires over the years. The larger tires are a big factor in the handling of the skirted-fender Fours, as these machines feel far more than thirty-six pounds heavier than the 1938s and 1939s. Also, as men-

A Four of 1932-1934 vintage. The bent Ace-style pushrods are evident. This is an authentic restoration; a minor deviation is the lack of a tire pump mounted above the chainguard. *Sam Hotton*

Riding a 1939 Four

It sits there on the side stand, idling as smoothly as your car, rocking slightly left and right from the torque reaction of the north-south crankshaft. A steady baritone burble leaves the exhaust, backed up by the hushed clicking of the valve gear. Air hisses through the carburetor.

The owner straddles the Four, and continues his briefing. The owner points out that the clutch isn't like that on other Indians. This is a single-pedal, spring-returned clutch, like something that belongs in a car. The owner shows you how to plant your heel on the floorboard with the clutch pedal depressed, so you can pivot on the heel when releasing the pedal. The owner goes over the controls and the shift pattern: back for low, forward for neutral, second and third (high) The bike is turned over to you.

You get on board, do the obligatory bounces in the saddle and twist the throttle. Wow! Lots of torque reaction makes the Four lean to the left. You nudge the kickstand up, depress the clutch pedal sharply against the spring tension and jerk the shift lever back into low. Clunk. Easing up on the clutch and adding a dash of throttle, you feel the side-rocking torque as you get rolling, but the torque reaction is slight when matched with the delivered power. You let the revs climb up to the mid-range, declutch, move the lever into neutral, hesitate and push forward to second. Ouch! Another clunk. Again the revs, again the pedal and lever game, again a clunk, but quieter. Now you're at 40 mph.

You remember the owner told you that first and third gears will always clunk because in those gears you're shifting dogs. But shifting into second gear calls for meshing gear teeth with gear teeth. This is where practice makes perfect. Over the next few blocks of stop and go traffic, you get six tries at shifting smoothly into second. You succeed once, sort of. It's all in the rhythm, the owner told you, and in the practice.

You're in the country now, speed at a steady 60 mph. You're disappointed; the motor is too smooth and too quiet. Here comes a hill, and you roll on a little more throttle. Above the slight rustle of moving parts you hear the carburetor hiss, while out back the added throttle makes the exhaust noise noticeable. On the level again, you back off the throttle and the carburetor hiss and exhaust noise are gone. When you back off, you also notice the first thing you'd call vibration, nothing bad but just a slight low-freqency encroachment on the smoothness. You slow to thirty, and can hear the exhaust better without the rush of air around your helmet. That's better.

Back up to 60, then 65 mph. There's little noise other than the air dancing around your face shield, rather like being in a sailplane, you imagine. You turn your head to the side so you can hear the exhaust, linger a moment, and then turn back to the front and the motorless wind. Now and then, you play with the throttle so you can hear the deep exhaust note come in with the call for more power.

You take it up to 70 mph. Hey, there's a motor down there! At a steady throttle setting you feel the low-frequency rumble that had earlier been confined to backing off the gas. At a steady 70 mph you can feel the motor, and at a steady 40 mph and below you can hear the motor, but in between it's touch and go to know there's a motor doing anything. Between 40 and 70 there's little to be felt. Too sterile, you conclude.

Without the distraction of a motor, you concentrate on the handling. The Four handles well, especially when compared to a Chief. Although ten pounds heavier than the twin-cylinder Chief, the Four has a lower silhouette, giving the false impression that the multi is significantly lighter than the big twin. You try some meandering in second gear at twenty, and find the Four easier to ride slowly than either the Chief or the Sport Scout. Of course, it's not as good a slow-goer as the 101. Steady and predictable is the verdict for the Four.

You return to a 60 mph pace. The bars don't vibrate, in the normal sense of the word; your hands feel like they're touching a hi-fi stereo. There's something "alive" in there. You could call it a hum.

You return the Four, and try to explain your mixed feelings to the owner. You're supposed to be ecstatic about the bike, so you're embarrassed that you aren't.

The owner nods, and explains that this is a motorcycle with two personalities. Cruising around the parking lot of an antique motorcycle meet, at idle or putting along, this baby makes motorcycling's king of sounds. The long stroke, the side-mounted exhaust valves, the combustion chamber shape, the minimal

continued on page 100

99

continued from page 99

muffler and the 78 ci all figure in somehow to produce the lowest pitch you've ever heard from a four-cylinder motorcycle. An Indian Four sounds more like a four-cylinder sports car than a motorcycle. Or maybe like a big inboard Chris Craft. The Four is the greatest motorcycle showpiece, the Duesenberg of motorcycling.

Then there's the personality you didn't capture in a short ride, the owner says. That too smooth, too quiet boredom gets better after an hour on the road. After two hours, better becomes a blessing. This is the ultimate old motorcycle for touring. With an oil cooler and modified oil passages, a late Four like this can cruise all day at 70. Out on the road, for a twelve-hour day, this motorcycle can't be touched by anything else older than a Gold Wing.

So, the owner summarizes, you can have your cake and eat it too. You have all the good show-off features, and you have all the practicality you need for serious touring.

tioned previously, the rear springing didn't work as well with the fat tires as with the original 4.50x18 tires.

During the war years, Indian built two experimental inline four-cylinder engines with all overhead valves. One of these engines was installed in a frame and road-tested. The other engine blew up on the test stand. Development was never completed, however, because of wartime priorities. At last report, the overhead Indian Four was still owned by Brooklyn, New York, enthusiast Clinton Feld.

Although a part of the verticals story in the next chapter, for continuity the Torque Four is mentioned. The Torque Four was

A 1935 Four. Being the first year of streamlined fenders and the last year of the Ace engine gives this model a unique character. Nonstandard items include white seat, handlebars, chromed wheels, and other bits and pieces. *George Hays*

Model 436, the 1936 "upside-down" Indian Four. Deviations from standard trim include chromed exhaust heat shield and an intake manifold shield. Restoration by Ray Hook.

one of three modular designs developed by the Torque Engineering firm, the series was to consist of a 10.5 ci single, a 21 ci vertical twin, and a 42 ci in-line four. Later in the development, the single and the twin were increased to 13 and 26 ci. This was the last four connected with Indian, but never advanced beyond the prototype form due to the pressing production problems of the companion singles and twins. Three of the Torque Fours were built.

Ownership

In April 1985, my friend Max Bubeck and I were heading north from Los Angeles on our old motorcycles along a lightly traveled road through the San Joaquin Valley. The delicious smell of orange blossoms along the roadside mingled with the motor's aroma in

a sort of contest for my approval. I approved of both.

I also approved of all the racket. As well as the galloping noise from my V-twin Chief, alongside me there was the hum of Bubeck's 1930 Indian Four. Every now and then I'd catch an extra dose of the Four's noise as Bubeck either increased or decreased the throttle setting.

Suddenly, a cloud of white smoke puffed from the breather tube of the Four, surrounding bike and rider. Bubeck slowed the Four slightly, so I passed him and looked back over my shoulder curiously. Then another white smoke eruption, as white and thick as steam. He slowed to a stop, so I turned around and rode back to find out what was the matter. From the old Four, the noise was now a calypso rhythm instead of a steady beat. Every thirty seconds or so, another white cloud would chuff from the crankcase. The verdict was clear: the Four had a hole in a piston. We limped along the remaining twenty miles into Tulare, an Indian twin and an Indian triple.

That night, around the dinner table with fellow Indian enthusiasts, I caught a quiet pause in the chatter. I recited the time-honored words: "You can't wear out an Indian Scout. . . ."

"But you can, an Indian Four," interrupted Lee Standley, a Sport Scout man. Everybody laughed. Well, everybody but Bubeck. The postmortem exam a few days later brought discomforting news: the piston with the hole was the rear one. I'd hoped another piston would be the problem. For the past year, Bubeck had been pumping me up with Indian Four talk, and backing up his words with thousands of miles of fast riding.

When you look at the right side of a Four, you have two reactions. First, you say to yourself, wow, look at those lines! Then, you

add, but too bad about those rear cylinders being starved for air; you probably can't run those beauties over 50 for very long. Everyone who ever purchased an Indian Four probably bought it in part because of the Four's great lines, and everyone who *didn't* buy one or who gave up on the Fours probably did so in part because of the rear cylinders.

It's obvious that the air supply is critical to the cooling of an air-cooled motor. When the British Vincent V-twin Rapide and Black Shadow were built, Philip Vincent said the rear cylinder was offset from the front in order to get more cooling air. Yamaha has said the same thing about their Virago V-twins. If the flow of air is that critical for V-twins, with all that open space between the cylinders, how much more critical must airflow be for an inline, north-south four?

Regardless of what Vincent and Yamaha have said, the fact is that the front cylinder of a V-twin is likely to run hotter than the rear, largely because the front cylinder tends to get less oil sling from the crankshaft. That's why some antique V-twins were equipped with extra external oil lines feed-

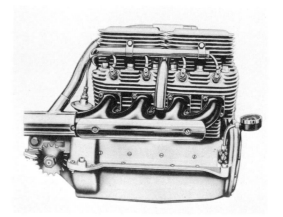

From the right-hand side, the 1938 and later Indian Four motor was one of the more aesthetically pleasing engines ever built. This factory publicity photo was done up in advance of production, and incorrectly positions the intake manifold heater (exhaust bypass). Closeness of transmission sprocket and clutch housing can result in a broken crankcase when a thrown chain is caught between the sprocket and case.

Sunburst cylinder head cooling fins are visible in this view of Ray Hook's 436. Left-hand shift could be fitted to new Indians. The tank paint scheme is nonstandard.

ing the front cylinder only. That's also why some Harley-Davidson oldies used to have problems with the front exhaust valve, but not with the rear exhaust valve. The point is, with the Four, many things aren't as they seem.

Everyone has heard or read stories about the Four, and passed them along. The stories are numerous, although almost all are related to two types of situations. The first story boasts that the Indian Four can run so hot that at night the pistons can be seen moving through the red glow of the cylinders. In the second, a guy runs his Indian Four at about 60 for an hour or so, and the thing locks up.

Let's talk about the glowing cylinders. A moment of rational thought deflates this yarn. If the cylinders glow red hot, they can be no hotter than the source of the heat, the internal parts. Internal parts that hot will seize up instead of moving around. Enough said.

OK, so there's such a thing as exaggeration with these Indian Four stories. How about the more believable story, the simple case of overheating after an hour or so at

A 1938 Four with optional standard tank panel. Dark pinstriping and white paint were extra-cost options. As in most Four restorations, intake-manifold-heater plumbing (exhaust by-pass) has been omitted. The manifold heater corroded rapidly due to condensation during cooldown. The flat black exhaust manifold is nonstandard; it should be black ceramic. *George Hays*

sixty? Here, we get into the gray area. There's no doubt that this happened to some Indian Fours; it's happened to V-twins so it surely can happen to Fours. The key question is, why did it happen?

When we talk about the why of it, we talk about air-cooled engines, and here we have a language problem. The term air-cooled is an oversimplification because all engines are cooled in part by oil. Actually, both the air-cooling and oil-cooling effects are comingled: too little air makes the oil's job tougher; too little oil, or oil that is too hot, can render any amount of air useless.

Back when motorcycle manufacturers bragged about dry-sump oiling, they attributed thirty percent of the cooling effect to the circulating oil. That, too, is an oversimplification, because the main purpose of oil is to supply a film between moving parts, the absence of which would produce local hotspots which cause fusing. Hence, the oil system takes care of the internal local area cooling needs. In so doing, the engine oil absorbs tremendous quantities of heat, heat which is dissipated around the engine by the moving oil. That heat passes through the engine surfaces, and is further dissipated by the primary engine-cooling medium, in this case, air. If the heat isn't adequately dissipated, the oil temperature rises to the point that the oil film breaks down and you get metal to metal contact and fusing. The engine locks up, in other words. All of this is touch and go; an engine might perform adequately "forever" at 60 mph on an eighty-degree day, but the same engine on the same day might tie up after fifteen minutes at 65.

So what about Bubeck's melted piston? He blamed this on inferior metallurgy. You have to use only the best pistons, he insisted, not just whatever you have. The breakdown was his fault, not the Four's, he added.

In 1986, Bubeck got his 1939 Indian Four restored, and the high-speed games have resumed. In the summer of 1987, he loafed the 1939 Four along at 55 mph so my 101 Scout and I could keep up on our ride from

The 1938 Fours offered battery ignition only; the magneto option reappeared in 1939. Seat trim, handgrips, and chrome bits and pieces are non-standard but authentic—just the way riders dolled up their bikes back then. *George Hays*

Palm Springs to Denver. Then, with me out of the way, Bubeck continued on to Pennsylvania, and finished off with a steady 70 mph return to California.

I confess to a few lingering doubts, but Bubeck's spirited riding has won me over to the Indian Four cause. As of this writing, I'm getting a 1938 Four restored, and it'll be a rider, not a show bike.

But let's face it, the Indian Fours that came out of the Springfield factory did overheat out on the open road. The quality of the road caught up with the quality of the design. Back in the twenties and early thirties, when there were few stretches of uninterrupted fast pavement, Four riders didn't have as many opportunities to find the limit of the Four's touch-and-go cooling capabilities. It's the long, steady fast grind that puts things into the twilight zone. Some had problems back then, but I think most of them occurred in motors that were running low on oil—not necessarily below the low mark on the dipstick, but just less than full. By the late thirties, there were plenty of opportunities to prove the Indian factory hadn't given adequate attention to the Four's cooling problem.

So why would anybody believe that Indian Fours can be ridden harder today than back in the thirties and forties? Because Max Bubeck has been conducting a long and—despite the one burned piston—successful experiment. And because Bubeck's Fours incorporate some homegrown tricks which make all the difference in the world.

Civilizing a Four for hard riding

By hard riding, I mean riding on freeways and keeping up with the crowd; cruising on the open road from Los Angeles to Phoenix at a steady 65-70 mph. In other words, a properly prepared and maintained Indian Four can be ridden in modern conditions with no more anxiety than you would ride any other motorcycle.

To begin with, you start with a five-main-bearing crankshaft. The three-main-bearing crankshaft of the Indian Ace and the Model 401 just isn't adequate. With the pre-1932 Fours, you need to be careful in assessing whether or not you're getting the five-main-bearing crankshaft, because the double

A 1941 Four. The angular bend of the rear fender brace was later changed to a more curved and graceful bend. The 1940 Indians had black headlights, old-style handgrips and thinner seats. Chrome tank strips were later added to the 1941 models. *Indian archives/Bob Finn*

down-tube frame doesn't guarantee the five-bearing shaft. On the right side of the five-main-bearing motor, five holes were drilled into the crankcase about three inches above the seam between the upper and lower crankcase halves. These holes were drilled to form the passageway between the fore-and-aft oil feed standpipe and the right-and-left oil feeds to each of the five main bearings. The front hole is covered by the oil gauge fitting, but the other four holes were

This 1940 Four offers a better look at the attractive crankcase. Period costume adds to the fun. *George Hays*

plugged with screws. Just count the screws; four screws mean a five-bearing crank and two screws mean a three-bearing crank. Before you buy, take a friend along or take a photo if in doubt.

The two most important modifications concern the oiling system. First, install a combination oil cooler and filter, or perhaps one of each. In Fours with the original clutch, use fifty-weight, single-viscosity oil in the summer and forty-weight in the winter; in Fours with the late-model Chalfant clutch use 20/50 in summer and 10/40 in winter; in Fours with the early Chalfant, use non-detergent oil of either multi or single viscosity.

Policemen liked Fours mainly for their easy starting, but smoothness was also praised. Among prewar state and provincial police organizations using Fours (numbers of Fours in parentheses) were Connecticut (145), Ohio (40) and Ontario (26). Chicago used 101 of the Fours. Lincoln, Nebraska, used 16 Fours, and the cities of Louisville and Indianapolis used many Fours as well as Chiefs. *Indian archives/ Bob Finn*

The next step is to finish the crankshaft manufacturing job that the Indian company left incomplete. The stock Indian Four crankshaft had a peculiar oil routing, left over from the early days when all Fours had a three-main-bearing crankshaft. When Indian went to a five-main-bearing crankshaft, they didn't bother to change the crankshaft oil plumbing. The number one main bearing fed oil through a drilled passage to the number one crank throw, thus lubricating the number one connecting rod. There was no drilled passage from the number two main bearing. The number three main bearing fed the numbers two and three rods. There was no drilled passage from the number four main bearing. The number five main bearing fed oil to the number four rod and the clutch pilot bearing.

As a result of the stock oil routing, there was likely to be an oil pressure drop toward the rear of the engine—the area facing the greatest cooling challenge. The cure is to take the crankshaft to a machinist and have passages drilled from the numbers two and four main bearings to the adjacent rods. In other words, when the work is finished there will be one continuous passage from the number one main bearing through the crankshaft to the other main bearings. This will tend to equalize the oil pressure throughout.

A critical step is to set up the engine clearances properly. Fit the engine with loose clearances; the slight amount of extra noise is a small price to pay for added insurance against locking up. Set up the numbers one and two exhaust valves with a clearance of 0.006 in. and the numbers three and four exhaust valves with 0.008 in. clearance. Set up the intake valves with 0.002 in. clearance, front to back. Also, install hardened exhaust valve seats.

If the Four is pre-1936, do the pushrod modification shown in the photo caption.

One point of careful maintenance is necessary: pay particular attention to chain and sprocket condition. There's not much room between the engine sprocket and the crankcase, so if you throw a chain you'll probably end up with a cracked or broken crankcase. Spare cases are as rare as honest politicians, and equally rare are the welders who might be able to patch up your mess. Use only the best chain available; keep it well oiled and adjusted. Watch sprocket wear closely, and when wear becomes evident change both front and rear sprockets as well as the chain.

The next modification should be done even if the plan to limit your Four to parking lots and neighborhood putts. Install a modified clutch by Earl Chalfant, either the early or late variant. The stock Indian Four clutch was a real grabber, so on cold mornings

yanking the bike into low would leave a one-foot streak of rubber on the pavement. The later Chalfant clutch features neoprene plates in lieu of the original metal to metal.

Thus equipped, an Indian Four is civilized.

To champion the cause of the Indian Four, Max Bubeck adds his perspective.

"My favorite Indian is the 1939 Four—like mine. It's comfortable and fun to ride. I've had mine almost fifty years now, and it has 137,000 miles on it. I bought it brand new in 1939 and rode it until 1953, at which time I parked it with 122,000 miles on it. I didn't

Owner Clinton Feld and his circa 1945 proto-type shaft-drive Four, designated the Model X44-1. All valves are overhead and the transmission is a foot shift. The engine has a one-piece barrel-style crankcase with a "door" in the front through which the crankshaft is inserted. Carburetor and air cleaner are concealed in a dummy left-side tank, perhaps the first use of the now-common dummy tank. *Emmett Moore*

know it, but the Four would stay parked until 1985.

"About Fours being fragile, that's true to a certain extent but they can be made to run hard and long if you do some work on them. The main problem with all the Fours was the lack of an oil cooler and filter, which I put on mine. In 1987, I rode my Four from Pennsylvania to California in four days, cruising at 70 mph. On the first day, I rode 754 miles in twelve and a half hours, which averages to a shade above 60 mph. I rode the total of 2,600 miles in four days, a 650 mile per day average, and I rode more than 600 miles each day."

General Prospects

In 1989, I greatly underestimated the price escalation of all Fours. Asking prices approximately doubled the projected top tier prices. In any case, all price estimates are exactly that—estimates. These estimates are provided to give you a general idea of what to expect.

1927-1928 Indian Ace,
1929 Model 401

There simply are too few of the Indian Aces and Model 401s around, so investment value and prices can't be predicted. Although I believe Indians should be ridden frequently, and on real trips, I acknowledge that many who buy Indians will find enjoyment without maintaining youthful riding habits. For such serious collectors, the three-bearing crankshaft isn't a major drawback despite its doubtful strength for long hard riding. Possibly, a three-bearing Four could be upgraded to a five-bearing job, but it would probably be cheaper to buy a five-bearing model in the first place.

The seller and the buyer of an Indian Ace or Model 401 will seldom have any recent and reliable information about the market consensus on these motorcycles. This is a risky scenario for both parties.

Circa 1947 prototype shaft-drive Four, which was to have been built along with the vertical twin Scouts and Arrow singles. The valve gear is the same as in the prototype twins and singles. Cylinder barrels and heads appear to be one-piece castings. Fenders are bigger and more stylized than production twins and singles. These fenders were incorporated on the 1952 standard Warriors. *Emmett Moore.*

1929-1931 Model 402

These bikes look and sound just as antiquey as the previous Fours. Yet, with simple modifications the 402s can be ridden seriously on the highway.

These early Fours, characterized by the between-the-rails fuel tank, have been undervalued in relation to the later Fours. Early Fours have been underpriced, partly because of the skirted-fender glamour and partly because people don't believe there's anything that can make any Four reliable, particularly the fragile-looking early Fours.

Prices for 402s should be 150-200 percent of the actual dealer's price of the Harley-Davidson FLHTC.

1932-1933 Model 403 and 1934 Model 434

I'll get into trouble here, as many—perhaps most—fans think these are better looking than the between-the-rails jobs. Not me. What's gained with the more shapely tank is lost with the front fender, and the extra ten percent of weight doesn't bring any advantages with it. To the contrary, handling is not quite as nimble as on the earlier Fours.

All this could change, if this book has any measurable impact on the market, but up to now, the public has been too willing to pay more for these than the earlier Fours. The investment cost for a restored Four of this year should be between ninety and one hundred percent of the comparison Harley.

Maybe Indian should've skipped the fancy prototypes and continued with this instead: a 1939 Four fitted with telescopic forks and modified lubrication system. The bike was bought new by Max Bubeck and has been ridden over 135,000 miles! For two-up riding, the jump is folded down, as shown, for the operator. The passenger gets the main seat. Bubeck rigged the 101 Scout-style gearshift for more positive control. Gearshift setup and lightened flywheel result in silent shifting—after sufficient practice. This motorcycle has logged thousands of miles in California enduros, through terrain just like this.

1935 Model 435

This was the first year of the stylish fenders, and a year before the unpopular upside-down series. I think these are a good bet despite their rarity, which makes cutting a deal riskier than with most Fours. Prices should be 150-200 percent of the actual dealer's prices of the Harley-Davidson FLHTC.

1936-1937 Model 436 and 437

The negatives have already been discussed. The upside-down Fours are another example of a serious collector model, one for rounding out the stable. If you start with a basket case, the total investment should be between ninety and 100 percent of the reference Harley-

Lots of Indians and Harley-Davidsons were fitted with these telescopic forks, built by the Vard company of Pasadena, California, in the late forties. The Flanders handlebars on risers used a quick-action left-hand throttle. These forks helped Bubeck with California's famed Greenhorn Enduro in 1947. The run was named for the Greenhorn Mountain, not for the few experts who could finish the course!

Davidson. The sale of a restored 1936 or 1937 Four has a scenario favoring the buyer, who should bargain hard because the seller expects it. Thus, there may be more of an opportunity here to get a good buy than with other Fours. Remember, if you buy and sell skillfully you can still break even in the long run.

1938-1942 Model 438-442

I lean toward the rigid-framed 1938s and 1939s, as I prefer their handling over that of the fat-tired skirted-fenders models. I like to feel clearly what the tires and the road are doing together. The springers are more comfortable, but that's another way of saying you can't feel as much. Most people disagree with me on this point, so you're on your own as to what good handling is all about.

As with the 1934s through the 1937s, the 1938s and 1939s also offer the owner the chance to be creative in selecting from an essentially limitless array of paint schemes. No matter what colors are selected, the end result will still be authentic.

An added plus is the price differential between the late rigid-framed Fours and the skirted-fender jobs. The investment cost for the perfectly restored 1938 and 1939 Fours should be between 150-200 percent of the reference Harley-Davidson.

The skirted-fender Fours sell themselves through styling. The only drawback to these visual masterpieces is the high price. You'll probably pay at least $2,000 more for one of these than a late rigid-frame Four, so you have to ask yourself if there's really that much difference. The money will come back to you, of course, so it's just a matter of how much money you want to park, and what kind of handling you prefer. Maybe the way to go with a skirted-fender Four is to fit the originally specified 4.50x18 tires, giving you something that's not only different, but also brings back some of the road sensitivity lost with the 5.00x16 tires.

The investment cost for a perfectly restored skirted-fender Four should be between 175 and 225 percent of the cost of the reference Harley-Davidson.

Chapter 5

★★	1949-1950 Arrow
★★↙	1949-1950 Scout
★★↙	1950-1951 Warrior
★★↙	1950-1952 Warrior TT
★★★	1952 Warrior
Not ratable	1952-1953 Patrol

Verticals 1949-1952

History
1949-1952

The history of the Indian Verticals is complex, involving a number of technical and financial matters. Sucher's *Iron Redskin* should be consulted by the serious student.

Briefly, these machines were designed outside of the Indian factory by former chief engineer G. Briggs Weaver. Industrialist Ralph B. Rogers decided to purchase the Indian company from E. Paul DuPont, and then have the Weaver design built at Indian

Circa 1946 prototype 21 ci, 350 cc vertical twin. The concept stayed the same but for production many components were changed, including the front forks, speedometer, headlight, taillight, cylinder head details, pushrod tubes, cam-case cover, oil tank, toolbox, exhaust pipes and mufflers. *Indian archives/Emmett Moore*

A 1949 Super Scout. Rocker arm enclosures differ from those of the prototype twin and four—they used horizontal instead of angular mating surfaces for the covers and head, prob- ably to facilitate manufacturing. Standard windshield has been removed. Believe it or not, this photo is from the Harley-Davidson archives! *Harley-Davidson*

and marketed through the large Indian dealer network. Rogers' idea was that a new breed of cleancut motorcyclists could be recruited by the lighter and more civilized looking verticals.

Although billed as 1949 models, the verticals were first sold in the summer of 1948. The offerings were the rigid-frame 220 cc Arrow single and the spring-frame 440 cc Scout vertical twin, models 149 and 249, respectively. The Model 149 single could be special-ordered with the same plunger rear suspension as the Model 249 twin. Several hundred Model 149Ms were sold to the Army. Because of continuing production problems, Chief production was halted during 1949 in order to concentrate on the verticals.

To give some appearance of a wider model range, the 249 Scouts were offered with three accessory equipment configurations: the basic Scout without accessories; the Sport Scout with rear view mirror, front crash guards, center stand and aluminum luggage rack; and the Super Scout, with added windshield, twin spotlights and rear crash guards, plus saddlebags in lieu of the luggage carrier. Fans of the famous V-twin Sport Scout considered the name misused on the vertical twin range. In the same manner, the singles were offered as the Arrow, the Silver Arrow and the Gold Arrow.

Total production of 1949 verticals— whether made in 1948 or 1949—was somewhere between 8,000 and 15,000 motorcycles according to most estimates. Adding the 1948 Chief output raises the total Indian production in this era to between 18,000 and 25,000 bikes. By comparison, Harley-Davidson built over 55,000 motorcycles during these same two years. British motorcycle imports totaled about 5,000 for 1949.

For the 1950 season, a few Arrow singles were offered as the Model 1150. These were leftover Arrows from the 1949 year, as Arrow production was already over. Likewise, a few leftover 440 cc Scouts were offered early in the season as Model 2250s. Most 1950 twins were the 500 cc jobs, however, either the Model 250 Warrior or the Warrior TT.

Year and model . . . . 1949 Arrow			

Year and model . . . . 1949 Arrow
  1949 Scout
  1950-1952 Warrior
  1950-1952 TT Warrior
Engine . . . .   Arrow: overhead-valve single-cylinder
others: overhead-valve vertical twin-cylinder
Bore and stroke . . . .   Arrow and Scout: 2⅜x3 in.
Warrior and TT Warrior: 2.54x3 in.
Displacement . . . . Arrow: 13.3 ci
  Scout: 26.6 ci
  Warrior and Warrior TT: 30.4 ci
Bhp . . . . Arrow: 10 (est.)
  Scout: 20 (est.)
  Warrior: 25 (est.)
  Warrior TT: 29 (advertised)
Gearbox . . . .   all: four-speed, foot shift on left side
Wheelbase . . . . all: 51 in.
Wheels . . . . . .   18 in., except some Warrior TTs with 19 in.
Tire, front 1949-1950: 3.25x18.00; 1951-1952; 3.50x18;
  Note: some Warrior TTs were equipped with 3.25x18 front

Tire, rear . . . .   1949-1952 Arrow, Scout, Warrior:
  3.25x18.00; 1951-1952; Warrior TT 3.50x19
Suspension, front . . . all: hydraulically damped telescopic
  fork
Suspension, rear . . . . . Arrow: rigid or optional coil spring
  plungers; Warrior, coil spring plungers or optional rigid
  others: coil spring plungers
Weight . . . .   Arrow: 245 lb. (dry, rigid-frame or
  spring-frame option not specified)
  Scout: 280 lb. (dry)
  Warrior: 315 lb. (wet, est.)
  Warrior TT: 300 lb. (wet, *Cycle* road test, Jan 1951)
Seat height . . . .   Scout and Arrow, 27 in.; Warrior 28.5 in.;
  Warrior TT, 29.8 in.
Mpg . . . . Arrow: 60 mpg (est.)
  others: 50 mpg (est.)
Top speed . . . . Arrow: 55 mph (est.)
  Scout: 85 mph (est.)
  Warrior: 90 mph (est.)
  Warrior TT: 80 mph (est., off-road gearing)

There were several improvements for 1950. An anchor stud was attached through the left side of the gearbox to secure the transmission against the frame tube under the seat. This eliminated gearbox vibration and attributed failures. The unusual 1949 cross-two-spoke wheels were replaced by conventional cross-four-spoke wheels. Provision for primary-chain adjustment was made via a shoe in the primary case.

Late in 1950, the Warrior TT was introduced as a 1950 model. The Warrior TT featured higher ground clearance, longer travel on the front forks, higher seat mounting,

A 1949 Arrow. Relax and enjoy the sport—no need to restore your Indian right away, or re-restore it. This older restoration by Ed Carlson could almost win best-unrestored trophies if Ed wasn't honest. Original forks were painted to match frame, tank and fenders.

western-style high handlebars, cadmium-plated instead of chrome-plated wheels with wider rims to accept 3.50 tires, high-rise exhaust system and optional lighting.

Some Warrior TT design changes focused on preventing water damage. The Warrior TT magneto was made water-resistant by sealing up holes around the cap. To prevent internal condensation, a vent tube exited under the gas tank. The high-tension wires were fitted with a moisture-resisting terminal. A different vent valve was used on the Warrior TT transmission. The regular gearbox vent valve was a breather, but the TT vent valve had a check action to keep water out when fording streams.

A forty-two-tooth rear sprocket was used on the TT model, instead of the standard forty-one-tooth sprocket. Rear sprocket options varied from forty to forty-seven teeth. Rear sprockets were screwed to the drum instead of riveted, so that sprockets could be readily changed. The transmission

sprocket was a seventeen-tooth instead of the standard nineteen-tooth.

To increase ground clearance, the front and rear of the Warrior TT were raised. Warrior TT front forks were one and a half inches longer, and slightly heavier fork springs also boosted clearance. The rear frame was made one inch taller by fitting a slipper bracket above the rear axle and a shorter spring below the axle. As a result, seven inches of ground clearance was obtained. Folding footpegs and a different bend to the brake pedal also enhanced rough going.

The Warrior TT engine was the same as the regular model with no special polishing or tuning except that pushrod seals were different. The Warrior TT compression ratio was boosted from 7:1 to 7.5:1. A ⅜ in. rear chain was fitted instead of a ¼ in.

During 1951, battery ignition conversion kits were supplied to dealers. There was no

A 1949 Scout currently campaigned in vintage racing. Special "cigar-box" oil tank was fitted by the factory to the team bikes for the 1948 Laconia 100 mile road race. A seat from a Benelli has replaced the original Indian bench seat. Exhaust pipes are nonstandard. Restoration by Bob Shingler.

lightweight American-made single; instead, the Indian Sales Corporation imported the Indian Brave 15 ci side-valve single built in England. The Brave is discussed in the next chapter.

The Warrior and Warrior TT were last offered in 1952. Apparently, few 1952 Warriors were built, as I've never seen a 1952 touring Warrior at any antique motorcycle meet, nor have I heard of one showing up at any of the meets of the Antique Motorcycle Club of America in the past twenty-five years. These 1952 Warriors were distinguished by Chief-style rear fender braces, Chief-style upper front fork panel, more deeply valanced front and rear fenders, chrome saddle spring covers and new fuel tank pinstriping.

The last verticals built were 1952 and 1953 three-wheelers known as the Indian Patrol. The Patrol featured electric starting and a Spicer standard differential. A Borg-

Warner single-plate clutch transmitted the Warrior-motor through a three-speed-and-reverse Borg-Warner hand-shift transmission and a shaft-drive. Colors offered were

In 1949, Indian bought motorscooters from the Lowther Manufacturing Company of Joliet, Illinois, and marketed them as Indians. The scooters had a left-foot clutch and right-foot accelerator. Twenty-four models were offered, including both two- and three-wheelers.

A 1949 Super Scout minus windshield and spotlights. Vertical twin engines were beautiful. Close-pitched fins were unusual for the era—they helped cooling but amplified motor noises. Carburetor room was limited, making twin carburetors impractical. The solo seat was super comfortable. Nonstandard trim includes paint scheme and chrome upper fork tubes.

Riding a 1949 vertical twin

This time, there's no need for a long briefing on the Indian you're about to ride; the owner simply points out that the controls on this 1949 Indian Scout are the same as you're accustomed to on modern bikes. The left-side foot shift and left-hand clutch make this job seem very un-Indian. The verticals were the only bikes back then that featured left-side shift with down for low, which has now become the universal pattern.

Here's where the first vertical oddity comes in: it has a left-side kickstarter like the Indian Four and the little side-valve singles and twins of a previous generation. You mention this to the owner, who says Indian was probably mainly interested in getting the shift on the left and the brake on the right in accord with American practice. British bikes of the period had right-side shifts and left-side brakes, which were never a big plus on this side of the Atlantic. British bikes were the new force in the marketplace of postwar America, so any kind of advantage over the Brits was important.

Before starting the Scout, you decide to give the bike your now-famous sit test. Giving the job a last look before swinging your right leg over, you see that the deeply padded solo seat is unusually shaped, more like a section of a horse saddle than the tractor style of previous Indian solo seats.

Your first impression is that the seat is incredibly comfortable, the best thing for your bottom since the 101 saddle. As soon as you move one foot to a footpeg, you realize the 1949 Scout sits small. If you didn't know better, you'd think this was a 125 cc bike built for teenagers. Again you comment, and again the owner has a point to make, saying that Indian offered an optional seat mounting that raised the seat one and a half inches for taller riders—Indian didn't get around to that option until 1950, however. You twist the handlebars right and left, bounce up and down in the deeply padded seat, then plant both feet on the ground and lean the motorcycle to the left and right. The point keeps coming home: this is a small motorcycle. You can imagine that riders less than five feet nine inches tall probably liked this, but larger riders probably felt cramped after riding the older and larger Indians.

The owner says he's installed a battery ignition, with the breaker points being hidden away inside the dummy magneto. Many vertical twins are modified this way.

The owner points out that the starting drill isn't as elaborate as theorized back in 1949. After listening to the starting explanation, you rise from the saddle and attempt to give the Scout a practice kick while astride the motorcycle. This feels too awkward, so you dismount to the left side in order to prod the kickstarter with your right foot. You push down the button on top of the carburetor until the gas runs out of the overflow vent. With the key off, you kick twice to get some vapors in the cylinders. You turn on the ignition key, open the throttle about one-quarter of a turn, and kick smartly. The vertical twin roars to life.

There's an average amount of tappet noise for a pushrod motor with aluminum alloy cylinder heads and barrels. The vertical sounds about like a Triumph of the era. You half expected gear whine, but there isn't any. When you comment on this, the owner responds that any properly restored vertical should be this quiet.

You're embarrassed by the thought, but this Indian feels kind of like an old Honda 350 twin. You blip the throttle, and the similarity ends; the 435 cc motor puts out as healthy a growl as any 500 cc.

You and the owner continue your small talk, until you conclude that the bike is warm enough. The steady clickity-clickity-clickity is pleasant, but it's time to roll. Then, it's in with the clutch lever and down on the foot shift, and your everyday riding reflexes get you rolling without any questions. This is the most relaxed Indian ride you've had. Around the residential area, you go up and down through the gears with hardly any mental effort. Now, into a less crowded neighborhood, now, you leave the Scout in fourth (high) gear at 30 mph, a relaxed pace which magnifies the enjoyment of the even firing intervals of a vertical twin.

Without distractions, you begin to think about the 1949 Scout. This is a tough Indian to judge. You keep comparing the Scout to the Hondas you've ridden, noting that the Indian has a nimbler feel than Japanese vertical twins because the American job is about sixty or seventy pounds lighter. The lower silhouette helps, too. But the Indian doesn't have the same solid feel down there in the motor, that overhead-cam feeling that suggests you can run the motorcycle right up to redline without a worry. The forks also don't seem to have as much damping as what you've experienced in other vertical twins. The rear springs work well enough, until your 30 mph clip takes you across a dip that makes the limited spring travel apparent. Past the dip, the springs continue to softly bounce a couple of times.

Hey, wait a minute! You realize your thinking is on the wrong track. This is a 1949 Indian, and as such, the little twin should be compared to previous Indians and to other 1949 creations. With your mind back in 1949, you appreciate the Scout's soft suspension.

Meanwhile, you've reached a wide boulevard which permits the Scout to be held at a steady 45 mph in fourth gear. This is a pace that's neither charming nor bothersome—call this business as usual. You slow down to enter a freeway, downshifting to third and then second, and then for the first time you roll on full throttle. Winding out in second, for a moment you feel the vertical twin get on the cam at about 40, with the extra kick that offsets the buzzing. You hit third at 50. You really hold open the wick in third, letting the little twin buzz to about 68, and feel the cam action again, although the gear ratio gives you more of a pushed than a kicked sensation.

Riding at 70 in fourth is too hard on the body. After all, this is a vertical twin without a modern gear-driven counter-balancer. You stick with the 70 mph pace for a couple of minutes to see if you get used to it, but you don't. You slow to 65, which only seems good because you've been doing 70. Then you try 60 mph. You can live with this, but the freeway drivers can't, so you ease over into the slow lane. With a lull in the traffic, you slow to 55 mph, and the motor seems to say thanks.

Off the freeway, now, you find that wide boulevard that leads back toward the owner's place, and you settle into a steady 45 mph clip. The feel that was businesslike in the first few minutes now seems more comfortable. You were too used to Indian V-twins when the ride started, you decide. The little Scout is busy but happy. Soon, you're at 30 in the neighborhood, pottering along with a smile on your face. Pulling in the owner's driveway, you wonder what to say after thank you. This is a puzzling Indian.

Indian Red and Police Gray. About 50 Patrols were sold, mostly to police departments.

Ownership

The Indian verticals, also known as the Torque series, are a study in contrast. The history of the lightweights "pushed" by Indian president Ralph Rogers, is a sad story full of might-have-beens, a history which I suspect begins to wear on many owners, since some collectors of other Indians look down their noses at the verticals. After all, these were the motorcycles that plagued Indian—some even say the verticals killed Indian, but Indian was already weak and the verticals' demise involved politics as well as engineering.

Most of the technical problems which damaged the verticals' reputation were solved by the Indian company. The other big blow to the Torques was uncompetitive pricing, and that is irrelevant for today's collectors.

How a bad reputation was earned

Let's be frank. In their original trim, these were bad motorcycles. Take the wheels— please! A peculiar wheel design was used in 1949. The 1949 wheels were an oddball size which forced the owner to buy tires from the Indian dealer. Not only that, but the spoke pattern was in defiance of fifty years of experience. Instead of crossing four spokes like on other motorcycles, the Torques crossed only two. As a result, the spoke loads weren't as evenly distributed and hard off-road riding would rip the spokes from the wheels. Sports-minded owners quickly learned, and laced Sport Scout rims to the hubs, restoring the standard spoke lace pattern. Conventional wheel rims were brought out in 1950.

Faced with rising costs of labor and materials, and the extreme expense of an idle factory, Rogers rushed the verticals into production before all the bugs had been worked out. A case in point is the primary drive chain, which in the original shipments had no means of adjustment. In a move that today would bring the government into the act for false advertising, Indian literature described the primary drive chain as "pre-stretched." Think about it. How can a chain be pre-stretched? Are the links farther apart than the sprocket teeth? Would this do anything at all toward extending the life of the chain over that of an ordinary one?

The initial Torque singles and twins were known for the crankcases filling up with oil after the motorcycles had been sitting for a few days, and in some cases when the motorcycles had been unused for as little as twelve hours. Dealers were advised to use a hammer and punch on the check valve between the oil tank and the oil pump, in order to seat the valve.

Engine tune-up specifications hadn't been thoroughly proofed prior to initial shipments, either. When owners complained that the Verticals didn't run smoothly at low speeds, a factory investigation resulted in new settings for the spark plug gap, the magneto point gap and valve clearances.

Probably the most common problem with the Torques was poor starting of the twins. Otherwise mild-mannered veteran motorcyclists can be moved to instant profanity by being reminded of their Vertical twin kicking days. Some note that it helped to live at the top of a steep hill. Both the singles and the twins used the same magneto, but in the case of the twin the sparks were routed through a distributor. The little magneto just wasn't strong enough to overcome the extra resistance of the distributor. Factory engineer James Hill related that the prototype vertical twins had a better magneto which was discarded in favor of the cheaper production type; Rogers was under pressure to get costs down.

For both the singles and the twins, poor starting could also result from carburetor air leaks in the choke mechanism. Dealers were

A 1950 Warrior TT built up from all new parts by Bob Shingler. The public commonly reversed the factory name to "TT Warrior." Standard forks were black. Cadmium wheels are correct stock items. Seat was raised 1½ in. over the standard Warrior by new mounting hardware. *Bob Shingler*

advised to seal air sources with solder, cork and shellac, and to modify the choke disc with saw cuts and pliers. Detailed starting instructions were issued to dealers, and these included the advisability of leaning the motorcycles slightly to the right, away from the rider who was attacking the left-side kickstarter, so that the carburetor would do a better job of drawing up the gas.

Some of the unsolved problems had nothing to do with the design, but were management matters which allowed the factory to build the Verticals without conforming to the design specifications. For example, the first 1,660 Model 149 singles and the first 268 Model 249 twins were assembled without filling the wheel hubs with grease. Then, to show you just how bad the production management was, after assembling several hundred twins correctly, this problem reappeared on Model 249 from serial number 2000 through 2047!

According to company documents, a number of Model 149 singles were shipped without removing welding flux and acid

Rider's view of Warrior TT. According to Indian advertising, more nonprofessional TT races were won on Warrior TTs than on any other bike during 1951.

A 1950 Warrior TT. The factory changed the road model rear springing; more springing was added above the axle, less below, to increase ground clearance one inch. Front forks were lengthened 1½ in. *Bob Shingler*

from the gas and oil tanks. The oil tank problem was serious in that rust could clog up the oil passages with catastrophic results.

Another problem was that front forks were prone to leakage because of careless factory assembly. Dealers had to remove and replace gaskets because the factory had not kept dirt away from the sealing surfaces.

Very noisy valve cam drive could result from mismatching of drive gears. The factory contributed to this problem by changing the gear-tooth design, by not clearly identifying the two kinds of gears that had been produced, and by not keeping records as to which serial-numbered engines had which kind of cam gears. Early singles had cam gears with twenty-degree pitch angle, and later machines had a fourteen-and-a-half-degree pitch angle. Although these differing gears were packaged and shipped under different part numbers, the gears were not stamped with the numbers. Later gears were cadmium-plated and earlier gears weren't, but the cadmium plating became less obvious after the later gears had been used. Moreover, lack of good factory records resulted in a salt-and-pepper application of

the gear sets. Most singles between serial numbers 1001 and 3485 were equipped with twenty-degree teeth, but a few were supplied with fourteen-and-a-half-degree teeth.

Nearly all twins had the twenty-degree teeth, but the factory acknowledged they didn't know the serial numbers of a few twins that had the fourteen-and-a-half-degree teeth. The way out of this mess was for mechanics to lay a one-sixteenth-inch diameter drill between the teeth of a gear. If the drill could be rocked between the gear teeth, it was a late fourteen-and-a-half-degree gear; if the drill fit tightly between the gear teeth, the gear was an early twenty-degree job. As the factory issued instructions on the matter, clearly some mismatching had already occurred at dealerships, resulting in a siren effect from the valve-train and more bad publicity for the beleaguered verticals.

On the 1948 verticals, valvetrain noise was sometimes caused by the assembly process in which cam-gear and breather-gear bearings were pressed into the aluminum crankcases. The internal diameters of these plain bearings were pre-drilled to the correct

A 1950 Warrior with Indian dual seat. *Bob Shingler*

120

size, but installation pressure could distort the bearings. In late 1948 this problem was solved by precision boring the bearing's internal diameters after installation.

What about the uncompetitive pricing? The reason for this was complex, having to do with the post-World War II inflationary economy. Simply put, Indian was unable to compete with larger companies for scarce capital, labor and material.

Among the many production problems faced by Rogers was the full automation of the manufacturing and assembly line parts conveyors. After considerable effort, the goal of conveyor automation was finally abandoned, so that Rogers' new one-story plant in east Springfield never lived up to its expectations as a cost saver.

Another cost problem was the increased use of subcontractors for manufacturing major items such as transmissions. Indian found that they could control neither the cost nor the quality of these suppliers. In a

booming economy, this made Indian a captive to its suppliers who were quite willing to drop their motorcycle sidelines in favor of more certain long-term projects. Rigid application of the factory quality inspection standards was causing horrible production back-ups, with the result that quality inspection standards were loosened so that motorcycles could be shipped to dealers. In turn, this put the Indian dealers and their customers in the quality inspection and engineering development business themselves.

The final and most serious cost problem for Indian was the devaluation of the British pound sterling in September 1949, lowering prices of British motorcycles twenty to thirty percent overnight.

Ralph Rogers wasn't so far off target with his idea of building motorcycles that would appeal to a new cleancut class of motorcyclists. After all, that's what Honda did a dozen years later. Unfortunately, Rogers didn't have the engineering and manufactur-

A 1951 Warrior. This particular motorcycle was hurriedly finished for the photo session, as the 1951 black tank panel doesn't quite cover up the 1950 Warrior TT trim underneath! Road model Warriors had the higher Warrior TT mounting for the solo saddle. *Indian archives/Ian Campbell*

A 1952 Police Warrior with floorboards instead of footpegs. The fenders are resurrected prototype Four items. The lower rear fender brace is now in the tubular Chief style instead of a flat strip. The rare 1952 Warrior (road model) used these fenders and braces, plus an upper fork panel like the 1952 Chiefs. *Indian archives/ Emmett Moore*

ing background to push the verticals through the intensive development required, in order to get the new motorcycles on the market before he ran out of credit. The Torques represented a good marketing idea, although most Indian fans would argue that Rogers' approach would have been better served by a lightweight derivative of the time-honored Sport Scout.

On the other hand . . .

The sad history of the verticals' launching doesn't have much to do with the quality of these motorcycles today. If you opt for a vertical, you won't be faced with ungreased wheel bearings, acid in the oil tank and unadjustable primary chains. The value of the British pound sterling and the sales appeal of British motorcycles are now irrelevant. The troublesome magneto may be repaired or discarded in favor of a battery and coil ignition disguised to look authentic. Repair consists of rewinding with heavier wire and installing a better condensor and coil, in other words, making the magneto like the original prototype unit.

So what do you have? The Arrow 220 cc single is perhaps just another lightweight, although with an unusual history. The vertical twins are something else. With the twins, you have a motorcycle concept that is different from anything available today, a concept which deservedly stands on its own merits. You have either a 440 cc or 500 cc twin-cylinder machine with the weight of a modern 200 cc street job, about 280 lb. plus gas and oil, for a total of about 315 lb. True, the pushrod design and small single carburetor place modern high rpm capability out of reach. In an all-out drag, an Indian vertical twin probably isn't any quicker than a 200 cc contemporary Japanese motorcycle, but how much more relaxing it is to shift at middle rpm, and in the real world of everyday riding that's what you usually do. Ridden this way, the Indian vertical twins compare well with the latest 500 cc double overhead cam wonders ridden in the same style.

The comeback is that the Indian vertical twins don't have modern features like electric starting, water cooling, swinging arm rear suspension and shaft drive. True enough, but in a classic case of "There ain't no free lunch," such features are why modern 500 cc street jobs weigh in at about 450 lb.

The Indian verticals' springing is crude by contemporary standards, but modern roads mean the limits of modern suspension systems are almost never challenged. Beyond that, the solo saddle of the verticals is infinitely superior to sitting on the typical sawhorse-shaped modern motorcycle seat. If your style of riding is mainly solo treks around town, plus an occasional leisurely paced tour, the easy handling of the verticals has a lot going for it. Putting it simply, riding a Torque twin doesn't constantly carry a

"weight tax" in the form of seldom used (or in some cases, never used) capabilities. For example, in 80,000 miles of riding, I've yet to ride my 550 cc double overhead cam Yamaha at redline. Add to that a suspension system that's never bottomed out. For my riding style, I'd be better off without the fancy hard-to-adjust-valve gear. Come to think of it, 150 lb. less rolling metal would be kind of nice. Perhaps that's why the Japanese lately have been offering a few large capacity but lightweight street singles.

Two owners report that their verticals have proven reliable racers. Bob Stark raced and later sponsored his vertical twin for twenty-three years of California racing. He says the only serious problem was caused by rider error during a road race: over-revving which put an exhaust valve through the piston. Bob Shingler, of Waxahachie, Texas,

A 1952 Warrior. One of few publicity photos ever published of this rare model.

has raced or sponsored two vertical twins and an Arrow for several years in the Historical Road Racing Association. Shingler reports that in over 1,000 miles of racing on his oldest vertical, there have been no lower-end problems and only occasional preventive top-end work has been required, as with any road racer.

To say a few words on the vertical twins, we again hear from Max Bubeck.

"The vertical twins needed a few things done to them, like the Fours did, but they were essentially a strong running engine for their size. I was very impressed the first time I rode a little 26 ci job. The biggest problem to get high performance out of them, was that the way the pushrods came up it restricted getting twin carburetors on them, unless you went to elaborate means. The

Triumphs, BSAs and similar English vertical twins had no such problem.

"The vertical twins had a good oiling system; they didn't seem to give any rod problems. The weakest reliability point on the verticals was the magneto—the ones that came on it. Then they built a few—I have one—that start the first kick and never give any trouble. My magneto is a two-spark. You can switch the spark plug wires and it doesn't make any difference. In both cylinders the spark plugs go off at the same time, but one of them is on the exhaust stroke so it doesn't make any difference.

"I won the 1950 Cactus Derby, about 425 miles of desert riding starting at midnight and ending the next afternoon. By 1955, with the plunger rear frame I was hard-pressed to keep up with riders using

Vertical twin dolled up in the classic American dresser style. Ugly stock dual seat has been replaced with this accessory seat. Restoration by Bob Stark. *George Hays*

swinging-arm suspensions, so I homemade my own swing-arm arrangement using Girling shocks. That brought the handling right back up to snuff again. It had excellent front forks, with six inches of travel available and variable damping, so with the new swing arm I could handle any type of terrain. Anyway, I won the 1962 Greenhorn 500-mile enduro with the swinging-arm vertical.

"In twenty years I put on a couple of thousand miles a year playing around off-road and riding in enduros. I made my own valve guides, and hard-chromed the intake valve stems to cut down on wear. I finally even hard-chromed the inside, the cylinder barrel, to eliminate wear. This was in the days before efficient air cleaners, so wear was a bigger concern then. I got it bullet-proof."

Prospects
1949-1950 Arrow

Arrows are mainly curiosities, with limited capabilities that restrict them to neighborhood jaunts. They are sought after primarily by those who wish to round out their collections. Restoration will cost nearly as much as the companion twins, which offer much

more performance. Prices of restored Arrows in 1988 were typically about $3,500 to $4,000.

1949-1950 Scout, 1950-1951 Warrior, 1950-1952 Warrior TT

As controversial motorcycles, all of the vertical twins are hard to rate. On the plus side, the verticals are American designed and built, and that should count for something. The twins are also the only American vertical twins ever built, a good talking point among collectors. The styling is beautiful, which is something you expect of Indians. For solo riding, these motorcycles are quite comfortable. The performance is satisfactory for many uses. Reliability is good, and they even start easily when equipped with coil ignition.

Since poor starting is so much a part of the vertical twin reputation, I'll emphasize the easy starting which is now typical by relating a true story. At Bob Stark's Starklite Cycles, a restored vertical twin had been sitting silent for four months. I watched Bob apply his starting technique of kicking the motor over twice with the ignition off, in

The last vertical twins were the 1952-1953 Patrol models. The machine featured Borg-Warner clutch and transmission, and Crosley automobile differential.

order to prime the cylinders. Then he turned on the ignition and kicked again, an action that produced a loud bark and a near start. On the next kick—the second kick with ignition after four months of storage—the vertical twin roared to life.

On the minus side, the verticals have a history that makes owners apologize, a history that is somewhat unclear. Many prospective buyers think these motorcycles are British built, partly because of the engine layout and partly because of Indian's later tie-in with the British Royal Enfield marque. The verticals neither look nor sound American. In my opinion, the stock control levers have a cheap feel, like something that belongs on a kid's toy instead of an adult's motorcycle.

There's no apparent rise in the demand for the Rogers twins. In 1988, beautifully restored verticals could be bought for $4,000 to $5,000, about thirty to fifty percent of the cost of our reference Harley-Davidson. This is the only way I recommend buying a vertical, fully restored, as the sellers are taking a drubbing at these prices. If you opt for a basket case and hire out the restoration labor, the total restoration cost won't be much different from that of a Chief—and Chiefs bring much higher prices on sale. In other words, if you hire out a Chief restoration you should break even or make a small profit (in inflation-adjusted dollars) upon sale, but in the same circumstances you'll lose big on a vertical. It's the old supply-and-demand game, and the verticals supply is greater than the demand.

A few people are buying these motorcycles with the idea that they'll have some fun while waiting for the demand to rise. In my opinion, they're still waiting—but they're having fun doing it.

1952 Warrior

The rarity calls the tune on this one. The fenders, fender braces, upper fork panels and seat spring covers were unique to this one year. I can't suggest a price range because I've never seen one of these for sale, but a break-even prediction seems safe.

One thing to remember about any of the Rogers motorcycles is that there's much less interest in any of them than in the more common Chief V-twins. Thus, whether you have a two-star, a two-and-a-half-star, or a three-star vertical, you may face a challenge in selling out someday.

Chapter 6

★	1951-1953 Brave
★★	1955-1959 Indian-labeled Royal Enfields
Not ratable	1968-1970 Indian-Horex, Indian-Norton and prototype (Munch) Sport Scout
★	1968-1983 Indian-labeled two-strokes and four-stroke moped
★★★★	1969-1970 Indian-Velocette

Imported Indians 1951-1983

History
1951-1960

The English firm Brockhouse began financing Indian in mid-1949, when Indian started importing several brands of English motorcycles to be sold in Indian dealerships.

A new marketing organization, Indian Sales, was formed to handle these English bikes which included AJS, Douglas (briefly), Excelsior, Matchless, Norton, Royal Enfield and Vincent. In early 1950, Brockhouse took control of Indian, and installed a new man-

A 1951 Brave 15 ci, 250 cc side-valve single. Economical but undistinguished, these English-built motorcycles were sold by Indian dealers from 1951 through 1953. *Indian archives/Emmett Moore*

Year and model .... 1951 Brave	Year and model .... 1955 Trailblazer
Engine .... one cylinder, side valve	Engine .... vertical twin, overhead valve
Bore and stroke .... 2.539×2.992 in. (64.5×76 mm)	Bore and stroke .... 2.756×3.543 in. (70×90 mm)
Displacement .... 15 ci, 248 cc	Displacement .... 42.27 ci, 692.72 cc
Bhp .... 10 (est.)	Bhp .... 42½ @ 5500 rpm
Gearbox .... three-speed, foot shift on left side	Gearbox .... four-speed, foot shift on right side
Wheelbase .... 52 in.	Wheelbase .... 54 in.
Wheels .... 18 in.	Wheels .... front, 19 in.; rear, 18 in.
Tires 3.25x18.00	Tires .... front, 3.50x19.00; rear, 4.00x18.00
Suspension ... front, hydraulically damped telescopic fork; rear, rigid	Suspension ... front, hydraulically damped telescopic fork; rear, swinging arm
Weight .... 247 lb. (dry)	Weight .... 405 lb.
Seat height .... 28 in.	Seat height .... 29½ in.
Mpg .... 82 in-town use (*Cycle*, July 1952)	Mpg .... 43, average town and country use (*Cycle*, May 1956)
Top speed ..... 68 mph, rider crouched (*Cycle*, July 1952)	Top speed .... 106.19 mph, rider crouched (*Cycle*, May 1956)
	Finish .... black frame; Indian red on tank, fenders, chainguard and toolbox

agement plan which included killing 220 cc single production and drastically reducing vertical twin production.

Lingering sales continued of leftover Arrow singles and vertical twin Scouts, and production of the Chief and vertical twin Warrior and Warrior TT also dribbled on. This chapter discusses foreign motorcycles that carried the Indian logo, not only for historical continuity but also to caution you that the name Indian on the tank doesn't

necessarily mean it's a genuine Indian made in the United States.

The devaluation of the British pound in September 1949 lowered Stateside prices of British motorcycles by about thirty percent overnight. This made life difficult for the Indian vertical twins, and absolutely killed any hope that the Arrow single could compete against imported lightweights. So, for

A 1955 Fire Arrow. This was the Royal Enfield 15 ci Clipper with Indian styling. Bore and stroke of 70 by 64.5 mm gave a displacement of 248.23 cc

or 15.15 ci; the claimed top speed was 70 mph. *Indian archives/Bob Finn*

the 1951 season, Indian dealers were able to offer the Brockhouse-built 250 cc side-valve single, dubbed the Indian Brave.

I'm tempted to say the Brave had nothing going for it except the Indian name and the price, but that's a little unfair. The economical manufacture of lightweight motorcycles has always been a tough challenge, and Brockhouse can be credited with doing a good job on this score. The suggested retail price of $443 in Los Angeles was only about twenty percent above America's top-of-the-line Cushman motorscooter, the latter pretty much a 1910 two-speed motorcycle with modern styling. The Brave styling was also

decent, and the Indian four-stroke lightweight gave more value for the money than the comparably priced Harley-Davidson 125 cc two-stroke.

The Brave didn't do well, however, possibly because shops that handled real motorcycles were handicapped when they tried to sell Mom and Dad on the idea of Junior riding a powered two-wheeler. Meanwhile, over in the motorscooter shops, parents were undisturbed by posters that glorified racing wins, and by the noises of big motorcycles. Scooters sold while the Brave didn't. The Brave was offered in the United States from 1951 through 1953 as a rigid-frame

A 1955 Woodsman. This was an off-road version of the 30.50 ci Royal Enfield Bullet. Bore and stroke of 84 by 90 mm gave a displacement of

498.76 cc or 30.44 ci; the claimed top speed was 85 mph. *Indian archives/Bob Finn* model. From 1954 on, the little bike featured swinging arm rear suspension, but was not imported by Indian Sales. Because of disappointing Brave sales, Brockhouse sold excess engines to the English Dot motorcycle company.

Beginning in 1954, Indian dealers offered only the Brockhouse-built Corgi folding minibike and Royal Enfield motorcycles. In 1955, the Royal Enfields sold in Indian shops were relabeled as Indians and featured minor styling touches in keeping with the Indian theme, as well as model names like Fire Arrow, Apache and Trailblazer.

For 1959, Indian dealers offered a so-called Chief, which was a 700 cc Royal Enfield twin equipped with 5.00x16 tires. This was the last year of the Royal Enfield charade, although a few unsold Enfield Indians were carried over into the 1960 production year and ultimately registered as 1960 machines.

1960-1963

Although no Indian-labeled motorcycles were forthcoming, for purposes of historical continuity I'll mention in passing the next phase of the Indian trademark. Associated Motorcycles (AMC) of Great Britain, manufacturers of AJS and Matchless motorcycles, bought the right to the Indian name in 1960. National headquarters remained in the Springfield, Massachusetts, area to keep up the connection with Indian's roots. The Indian dealerships then were renamed Matchless/Indian.

To their credit, AMC didn't bother to stick the Indian logo on any motorcycles. By this time, spare parts for American-built Indians were seldom requested, so the AMC regime cleared out all spare stocks for "real" Indians. The AMC connection lasted until late 1963, at which time the national distributorship for Matchless motorcycles passed into the hands of the Berliner Motor Corporation, and all references to the Indian name were dropped.

This marked the last period in which the Indian logo could be continuously traced from its historic beginnings.

A 1955 Tomahawk. This 30.50 ci, 500 cc vertical twin was known in Britain as the Royal Enfield twin—there was no official model name—until designated the Meteor Minor in 1958. The 70 by 64.5 mm bore and stroke gave a displacement of 496.45 cc or 30.30 ci. Top speed was about 90 mph.

1967-1983

During 1967, Floyd Clymer, former Indian west coast distributor, became associated with German Friedel Munch, who designed and built an 1100 cc inline four based on an air-cooled NSU automobile engine. Clymer handled the world distributorship of this Munch Mammoth, and Munch undertook design efforts of a Mammoth derivative powered by an Indian Sport Scout 45 ci engine.

For the Scout project, Clymer took four Indian experts to Germany with him to assist in finalizing a prototype. The Clymer team consisted of Frank Christian, Max Bubeck, Dick Gross and Art Hafer. Christian was one of the first successful builders of stroker Chiefs of more than 80 ci. Bubeck was the rider and co-builder with Frank Chase of the fastest-ever unstreamlined Indian, a Chout featuring a Chief engine in a 101 Scout frame. Gross was the designer and tuner of the special four-cam Indian Sport Scout ridden by Bobby Hill to numerous national championship titles during the 1950s. Hafer had built and tuned the Sport

A 1955 Trailblazer, known in Britain as the Royal Enfield Meteor 700. Bore and stroke of 70 by 90 mm gave a displacement of 692.72 cc or 42.27 ci.

The claimed top speed was 100 mph plus. This was the biggest seller in the Enfield Indian line. *Indian archives/Bob Finn*

Scout raced by Ernie Beckman, whose many victories included the last national championship racing title won on an Indian.

The Munch Sport Scout prototype was a smash hit at the Anaheim, California, motorcycle show in late 1967, but it never went into production.

In 1968, Clymer began to use the Indian logo on small two-stroke motorcycles. Operating out of Los Angeles, Clymer's idea was to keep the Indian name alive, while pursuing his dream of a new Indian motorcycle built around the Sport Scout motor. The Indian logo went on two minibikes: the Indian Ponybike powered by a 50 cc Czechoslova-

kian Jawa/CZ engine and the Indian Papoose powered by a 50 cc Italian Minarelli engine. Also, a Jawa/CZ powered Indian Boy Racer was marketed, making it the first miniature motorcycle designed for off-road riding by youngsters. By far the largest number of Clymer Indian-labeled two-wheelers were the two-stroke minibikes.

Orders didn't materialize for Clymer's cherished modern Sport Scout, so he arranged to have special Italian Tartarini frames and running gear combined with either the Velocette 500 cc single or the Royal Enield 750cc vertical twin, both revered British designs. There were 200 of the Indian-

Changing of the guard. In 1959, Indian Sales Corporation marketed the so-called Indian Chief, which was actually the Trailblazer fitted with 5.00x16 tires and minor trim changes. Concurrently, Indian Sales severed their Royal Enfield connection and began to import Matchless motorcycles, an example of which is shown here. Some 1959 Chiefs were sold in 1960 and titled as 1960 models. Factory engineer Jimmy Hill is with bowtie at extreme left. *Indian archives/Stephen Wright.*

Velocettes sold in the United States and fifty more were marketed through English dealer Geoff Dodkin. The number of Royal Enield-powered Indians built is unknown but believed to be less than ten. One or more Norton 750cc powered bikes were built.

Clymer one-offs included an Indian-labeled bike featuring the German Horex overhead cam twin engine and an electric minibike. Only one Indian -Horex is believed to have been built.

Because of Clymer's success in marketing Italian minibikes, in the minds of potential first-time purchasers the Indian name had become associated more with minibikes than with motorcycles. For this reason, upon Clymer's death in 1970, a Los Angeles lawyer purchased the Indian rights from Clymer's widow, in order to affix the Indian name to Taiwanese minibikes.

The new Indian Motorcycle Company was located in nearby Gardena, California. After importing a dribble of minibikes, the company established its own factory in Tai-wan, which included the largest motorcycle assembly line outside of Japan. About 20,000 minibikes were built in 1973; however, sales weren't forthcomng, and in 1976 this company declared bankruptcy.

The Indian logo was then sold to American Moped Associates of Irvine, California. This organization imported a four-stroke moped made in Taiwan from 1977 through 1981. The business world can be irreverent, but in naming the four-stroke moped the Indian Four, some sort of record of disrespect must have been established.

As the moped was phased out, the Indian logo was next affixed to a go-cart.

As of this writing, I don't know the exact status of the Indian name and logo, but I'd not be surprised if the revered old name shows up again on some two-wheeler far removed from the true Indian story.

Ownership and prospects 1951-1953 Indian Brave

Although the Brave wasn't built at the Indian factory, there's still a connection

The one and only 1968 Indian Scout by Clymer and Munch. the big-base Sport Scout design was modified for four-cam valve action, using Electron crankcases. Note the huge front drum brakes, alloy rims, and European styling to the bodywork. A radical departure from the old-guard Indians.

between the Brave and the "real" Indian motorcycle company. You could call the Brave a half-breed, a motorcycle built outside of the Indian factory but supplied to dealers who were still selling US-built Indians.

As yet, there hasn't been any noticeable interest in the Brave, and I think it's unlikely that these machines will earn their keep from an investment angle.

1955-1959 Indian-labeled Royal Enfields

The Enfield Indians have an even weaker connection to Indian history than the Brave, since during this era there was no American production of Indians. The Indian name steadily lost its marketing magic, as hopes faded for a revival of the American V-twin saga. Royal Enfields were acceptable but unexceptional motorcycles, with no earned heritage in the United States. Even on their home turf across the Atlantic, the marque didn't capture a hard-core band of super enthusiasts as did rival makes. With neither technical nor financial strength behind them, there was no instant glory to be won by Enfield Indians on the national racing circuit. Consequently, the motorcycles couldn't overcome the public resentment of the English Brockhouse organization's ownership of the grand old American marque.

Collector interest in other British motorcycles is growing, but I don't see this rubbing off on the Enfield Indians. As symbols of a sad time, I don't think the Indian-labeled Royal Enfield motorcycles are going to hold their own against inflation.

1968-1983 Clymer two-strokes and all mopeds

Why collect junk? Somehow, the Indian name makes this stuff even worse.

The gas tank tells the tale. This 1969 Indian-Velocette was expertly restored to a customer's specifications, which included placing the Velocette logo on the tank instead of the original Indian logo. In most eyes, the appeal of the Indian-Velocette is its Velocette connection rather than the linkup with promoter Floyd Clymer and his Indian theme. Classic big-single torque, state-of-the-art Italian running gear and Velocette heritage make this an interesting machine. *Richard Renstrom*

Circa 1968 Indian-Horex, another one-off. Smooth running for a twin of the era. The rider is former racing star Jody Nicholas. *George Hays*

1965-1969 Clymer four-strokes
1969-1970 Indian Velocette

None of the Clymer four-strokes were built in sufficient numbers to rate except for the Indian-Velocette. The bike is a sound investment because of the Velocette connection, and because the Indian-Velocette just happened to be a well-functioning motorcycle. Velocette is one of the more revered names among collectors of British motorcycles, and beyond that, a period road test termed the Indian-Velocette a better-handling bike than the genuine article. Ironically, the Velocette linkage rather than the Indian logo tells the tale.

```
Year and model ............... 1969 Indian-Velocette
Engine .............. single cylinder, overhead valve
Bore and stroke ............. 3.85×3.85 in. (86×86mm)
Displacement ..................... 30.45 ci, 499 cc
Bhp .................... Venom tune: 37 @ 6200 rpm
Thruxton tune: 41 @ 6200 rpm
Gearbox ........... four-speed, foot shift on right side
Wheelbase ................................. 56 in.
Wheels ..... 18 in. by Borrani; Grimeca twin leading-shoe
    front brake
Tires ................ front, 3.25x18.00 rear, 4.00x18.00
Suspension ... front, hydraulically damped telescopic fork
    by Marzocchi; rear, swinging arm
Weight ........................... 345 lb. (dry)
Seat height ................................ 32 in.
Mpg ........ 43, average town and country use (Cycle,
    May 1956)
Top speed ... 101 mph, indicated on Smith's speedometer
    (Cycle Guide, Dec. 1969)
Finish ... black frame. Options. black and metallic blue on
    tank battery cover and toolbox; metallic blue on fenders and
    chainguard; black and purple with same arrangement as in
    option one; bronze and white on tank, bronze on fenders,
    battery cover, toolbox and chainguard
```

Specials
1928-1969

History
1928-1969

Motorcyclists have always been individualistic, so the overwhelming majority of Indians were outfitted with accessories or stripped down for the racer look. Dressers were easier to create, since parts were simply bought at the Indian shop and bolted on.

Civilianized Model 841. The first such special was probably built not long after World War II, but popularity increased during the fifties when Indians were new to collectors. Most restorers of 841s now go for the military look. *George Hays*

Dealers got a big markup on the bolt-on goodies, and so they promoted this style more than the bobber genre.

From the 1930s on, countless Indian owners went the bobber route already discussed. In California, stock Indian fenders were considered too tame by young riders who either rode *sans* front fender or gave the hacksaw treatment to the original fender. In the Depression years, dealers hauled away Indian front fenders by the pickup truck load, depositing them in the local junkyard.

But for some Indian enthusiasts, individuality also meant mechanical changes, and the resulting specials. The term special should not be confused with chopper. The specials represented the views of Indian loyalists as to the kinds of motorcycles they thought the factory should have built. Style was important, but cosmetic changes were not made at the expense of functionality. One would

think twice these days about doing anything with an Indian other than restoring it to original trim, but attitudes were different then, as parts were more plentiful and cheaper.

Among the earliest and most popular specials were the so-called Chouts. A Chout consisted of a Chief engine in a 101 Scout frame. To shoehorn the motor into the frame, the builder had to bend the lower tank rail upward. The modified upper area was then concealed by a Junior Scout tank. In 1948, a Chout built by Frank Chase and Max Bubeck was ridden over 135 mph by Bubeck in unfavorable crosswinds. This was the fastest speed ever electrically timed for an unstreamlined Indian.

A few riders installed the deep-breathing and fast-turning Sport Scout engine into the good-handling 101 Scout frame. Others simply fitted Sport Scout barrels and heads

Adding a telescopic fork was a popular modification, although mostly done on Chiefs and Sport Scouts. This particular job is especially thorough, as rider Bob Stark has shortened the tall 1940-1941 steering head to the same dimensions as the postwar Chief steering head. Without this change, the forks would have insufficient rake and unstable steering. *George Hays*

to the engine of their 101 Scout. Most Sport Scouts were eventually stripped down by a succession of owners. The umpteenth owner of a by-then old Sport Scout sometimes had the extra motivation of saving money by not replacing or repairing damaged stock fenders.

In the last days of Indian as an American motorcycle manufacturer and over the decade following, the depth of Indian rider loyalty was revealed in a number of more complex specials. In the late 1950s, the later Indians were sought after not only as collect-ibles, but also because their pleasurable riding qualities made them at home on the contemporary scene. These period specials perhaps have a collectibility status all their own. A concern here could be the proof of whether machine X was actually built by well-known Indian fan "Joe" in 1959, or whether X was built last week at the local chopper shop.

The later specials included combinations built up from vertical twin frames and either Sport Scout or Chief engines. Another pop-

Former racer and tuner Lee Standley with his modified Sport Scout. It has a 1939 front frame section with 1941 springing, softened rear spring action, Warrior gas tank, and Royal Enfield forks and front brake. Crankcase pressure breathes into a six-inch standpipe (on opposite side) so the engine stays dry.

ular special was the civilized Model 841, complete with skirted fenders. One of the simplest and most functional changes was the substitution of a telescopic front fork for the earlier varieties. This began with the Vard fork of the immediate postwar era, and continued with later telescopics, often of Indian manufacture or supplied by Indian dealers.

The Sam Pierce creations are in a class of their own. An ardent California Indian dealer and former pitman to legendary Indian star Ed Kretz, Pierce poured a lot of money and time into two efforts at Indian production. In 1951 he completed a prototype 1952 American Rocket P-61. Power was furnished by a rubber-mounted Chief engine sleeved to $3\frac{1}{16}$ in. bore, and destroked to $3\frac{13}{16}$ in., giving 60.8 ci or 997.1 cc. Ford connecting rods were used in order to cut the cost of building a stronger bottom end than the stock Indian issue. The big-end bearings

were combination Ford plain-insert and commercially available double-row ball bearings. Mercury cylinder sleeves and pistons were fitted. The American Rocket was given a good sendoff by *Cycle* in the May 1952 issue. The cover photo showed a costumed space hero riding the motorcycle through the galaxy. Pierce planned to go into limited production at $995 each, but the project died.

Pierce's other go at Indian building began in 1967. From a large stock of Indian and Royal Enfield Indian parts, Pierce assembled a few dozen Sport Scouts in various custom finishes, and advertised them for $1,000 each. Some were equipped with a fancy fiberglass combination gas tank and seat; others were styled along traditional lines. All were customs. Motor sizes of 30.5, 37, 45 and 52 ci were offered.

Indian choppers are popular, but choppers came into vogue in the 1960s, and thus

The Dewey Bonkrud Sport Scout. This includes a vertical twin rear frame grafted to a Sport Scout front frame; diagonal and vertical rear struts were then added on. The cylinder heads are a rare prewar racing type. Other mechanicals are a Volkswagen generator and vertical twin forks. A more common variant is the Sport Scout motor in a complete vertical twin frame.

aren't part of the unbroken historical evolution of Indian. In any case, as highly individualistic creations, Indian choppers have no predictable investment value. You can count on one thing, however; Indian choppers have less value than stockers, dressers, Bobbers or period specials.

Ownership and prospects
1928-1969 Specials

As expressions of the often idealistic Indian riders, the period specials deserve preservation. Careful buying is in order, however, because some of these jobs represent considerable investments of time and money by their builders. Before buying, you'll need to make sure you're not buying some Johnny-come-lately homebrew, and make sure you can likewise convince your buyer someday. The authentic connection with an Indian personality—a dealer, a rider or a mechanic—is what gives these machines collectibility. Nevertheless, these motorcycles don't have a universally recognized status, and the profitable sale of one will require above-average salesmanship or a buyer who just happens to share your enthusiasm for the associated Indian personality.

The 1952 American Rocket P-61 prototype designed by the late Sam Pierce. Components include a Model 841 frame and gas tank, rubber-mounted Chief engine with Ford and Mercury components, and a foot-shift and hand-clutch setup resembling the prototype 1949 Chief. Total weight was 518 lb.

Dewey Bonkrud's Chout with a vertical twin front fork. The stretched vertical twin frame is built up from two separate frames, with extra bracing on the rear structure. The gas tank is from a Matchless. The crankcase with separate distributor and oil pump is early Chief; the barrels and heads are late Chief. Destroked to four inches, with standard bore, the engine is 66.4 ci or 1087.5 cc. In this 1984 shot, the Chout has finished a day of off-road riding, retracing some of the old Greenhorn Enduro route.

A 1968 Sam Pierce Sport Scout. Pierce sold
rebuilt Sport Scouts in 30.50, 37, 45 and 52 ci
versions, each for about $1,000. The tank is from
a Royal Enfield Indian; the tank badge was used
on later Enfield Indians. Rider is Paul Watts.
George Hays

Chapter 8

The Indian scene

Why Indians cost more

Indians became instant collector items in 1954 with the demise of the marque, yet parts were still easy to find. As of 1954, people stopped junking Indians, and those with 1953 Chiefs considered themselves lucky.

The same wasn't true for old Harley-Davidsons, however; by 1960, a 1953 Harley-Davidson was just an old motorcycle. A few smarter-than-average enthusiasts began collecting old Harleys during the 1950s, but they felt embarrassed enough to make excuses to their Indian-collecting friends. As a result of the shortsighted attitude shared by many collectors during the decade following Indian's collapse, Harley-Davidson collectors suffered through two decades of parts scarcity before specialists began remaking Harley hardware.

This never happened with Indians; either new-old-stock or remanufactured parts for American-built Indians have been available continuously since Indian quit production. At first, a few enterprising dealers bought up large stocks of Indian parts, sometimes by the ton. Then, specialist firms began remanufacturing a few unobtainable items, and upon sticking their figurative toes in the water, found business profitable for these motorcycles that were simultaneously collectibles and ridables. The happy outcome is that Indians, particularly the later Chiefs, are the most maintainable of any collectible motorcycles in the world.

On the down side, because Indian collecting became popular so many years before Harley-Davidson collecting, you'll find Indian prices higher than comparable Harley-Davidsons. Likewise, Indians cost more than old foreign motorcycles, with the exception of certain recognized foreign classics. The history of Indian collecting also means you aren't going to be able to pull an investment coup, and guess which models will be five-star investments. I've rated no Indians five stars because no Indian sellers are going to underestimate the value of their merchandise. But as I said at the outset, the investment angle is only one of the factors to consider in buying an Indian. On the other hand, it's difficult to lose money on an Indian. Even the few models I've called below average, with extra patience, can be bought and sold favorably.

Restoring and maintaining Indians

Since 1954, demand for parts has been worldwide and strong enough to foster growth in the Indian industry. Today, over half a dozen Indian parts firms have been in business for over twenty years. Hiring out your Indian restoration is no problem, either, as a number of shops across the country do Indian work; check the ads.

The most maintainable of the Indians are the Chiefs. All mechanical and electrical

Bob Finn trying his luck at a field meet circa
1953. A mistake means a wet rider. Bob's Chief
has typical Indian accessories. *Bob Finn*

parts are available either as new-old-stock or as reproduced items. In a few cases, suppliers have suffered through early quality problems with new items, but the bad stuff eventually gets weeded out. Generally, modern technology results in reproduced parts with higher quality than the originals. Cosmetic parts are being reproduced, either in metal or fiberglass. With a Chief, you have no more concern with maintenance

Thirty-four years later, here is the seventh annual California Indian Run in 1987. The squaw aims for the mustard-covered hot dog. Chief is World War II issue.

than with modern bikes—and sometimes even less concern.

Early Chiefs and Scouts—regular or Model 101—are harder to outfit with fenders than are the later Indians. However, most other Scout cosmetic hardware is being reproduced. Transmission gears are hard to obtain for the Scouts and 101 Scouts, but valves, pistons, bearings and other engine parts are readily available.

Sport Scout parts are rarer than Chief parts, particularly the 1940 and 1941 rear fenders and chainguard, each a one-year-only variety peculiar to the Sport Scout. Mechanical and electrical parts can generally be supplied. The transmission is no problem because it's the same as the Chief's except for the housing. Exhaust systems are rare, so if you want the stock appearance you'll probably have to go to the trouble or expense of fabricating the plumbing. Floorboard hardware is another headache, and this stuff usually has to be fabricated from scratch.

Today, restored Fours often work better than the factory-fresh originals. The infamous grabby clutch has been improved upon twice, first by the Chalfant clutch and later by the Young clutch. Transmission triple and sliding gears have been remanufactured. Some parts, however, are extremely rare, including crankcases and ring and pinion gears. Gas tanks are hard to come by too, so the standard route is to modify Chief or Sport Scout tanks. Cosmetic pieces are being reproduced.

Parts for the verticals are in fair supply. The northwestern United States had more than average sales of the Rogers lightweights, so look for ads in that area. Some dealers specialize in these parts.

The other Indians are in the collector-only status, so you can expect no dealer support for the earliest and rarest of Indians. A few parts on the Powerplus genre are common to the Chiefs, and the 1915 F-head transmission can use some Chief parts. Some parts

Squaw contests are a nice touch missing from Harley runs. Lil McClintock is owner and rider of this 1940 Four and sidecar.

can be swapped back and forth between the Prince singles, the 30.50 ci twins, the Powerplus singles and twins and the various Franklin-designed racers and hillclimbers of the 1920s. Research and persistence will reap dividends, but fabrication probably will still be necessary for some items.

Indian events and places

A few Indian-oriented events are sponsored each year in the antique motorcycle movement. In Springfield, Massachusetts, an annual Indian Day is held each summer on the grounds of the Indian Motorcycle Museum. The museum is located in part of the East Springfield Indian works purchased by the company prior to World War I. These buildings, incidentally, were also used for production of the verticals in the Rogers era. The museum, open year-round, is operated by Charles and Esta Manthos. Featured are the hand tools used by Oscar Hedstrom to

You don't have to wait for an organized run to participate. Just drop by and visit a fellow enthusiast. Richard Morris shows off his Indi- ans; this is only part of his collection of antique American motorcycles.

Is this happiness or what? *Sam Hotton*

construct the original Indian prototype, as well as some personal effects of George Hendee. Also on display are trophies won by Hedstrom at early events such as the 1906 Ormond Beach speed trials. A prototype Indian car, as well as a number of Indian motorcycles, are on exhibit.

As of this writing, half of the old State Street Indian plant is still standing in Springfield proper. A ride by gives a ghostly feeling.

In Ohio, the Indian Four Cylinder Club holds its annual rally. In California, two annual Indian events are held. The Bury The Hatchet Run is promoted by The Shop of Ventura, in which Indian riders host a poker run ridden by Harley-Davidson riders. In mid-California the annual Indian Day is held, which includes a Sam Pierce Memorial Road Run.

Chapter 9

The "new" Indian,
Indian Four horror stories, and more

Department Of Almost-Lost Arts; The Leaf Spring Fork And The Rigid Frame
Riding a 1938 Chief at a steady 50mph through the rolling hills of northern Victoria, Australia, I was getting nauseous. The two-lane asphalt road was uneven, and quilted with patches over patches over patches. Here

and there the front tire hit an unpatched hole and jarred the front end upward, sometimes lifting the wheel from the ground, always jolting the Chief frame and sending a shudder throughout my body.

The seat post springing was stiff enough to carry a 300lb policeman. I had often imag-

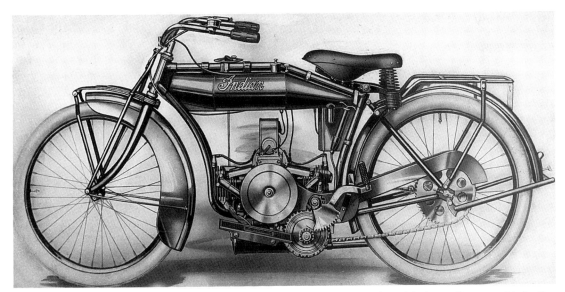

1918 Model O. For 1918, the Model O was equipped with a leaf spring fork. The Model O was last offered as a 1919 model. Oddly, at the moment Indian gave up on this concept, Harley-

Davidson introduced their small opposed twin, the Sport. It failed also. Indian Archives original from the Jimmy Hill collection, copied by Earl Bentley (hereafter, Hill/Bentley)

Example of an improperly setup leaf spring fork. Although the motorcycle is unloaded, the rockers are nearly horizontal. The nearly horizontal position of the rockers causes three bad effects. First, there is no fore-and-aft cushioning because the wheel has no rearward motion left. Second, the rocker is perpendicular to the bellcrank (rods connecting to the leaf spring). This means that the leaf spring is offering maximum resistance to the wheel movement. Third, there is very little upward movement available. Properly setup leaf spring forks have the rockers at an angle of thirty to forty degrees. Check Indian archives photos throughout the book for several examples of correct geometry.

ined that a lot of them stopped at every roadside diner. Perhaps this was proof.

I began to watch the leaf spring fork. The fork moved (but did little to absorb) the larger bumps and holes. I quickly took up the habit of rising off the seat for these visible jolts. But the majority of the bumps and holes weren't visible at 50mph, and there was no way to offset the punching, snapping, pounding, and throbbing misery. Good grief! The forks moved little if at all on these bumps!

How could a 1938 Chief fork move so little? After all, I'd ridden several thousand miles on a 1929 Scout, and often relieved boredom by watching the Scout's leaf spring fork move slightly up and down on even the smoothest road, absorbing every little bump and blister. Sometime between 1929 and 1938, did Indian forget how to make a leaf spring fork work? I don't think so.

At the next rally rest stop, my old buddy Max Bubeck borrowed a tire gauge. The 1938 Chief was carrying about 30psi in the rear tire and 26psi in the front tire. "You should be running about 22psi in both," Max said. With the tire pressures corrected, there was a big improvement. Still, the Chief remained a rough rider.

After the rally, we concluded the following: Taking the simplest problem first, you should ensure your seat post springing is properly adjusted. When you sit on the motorcycle, the seat should settle down about an inch and stay there. This is extremely important because the seat suspension is ninety percent of the rear "suspension" on a rigid frame machine. With the proper saddle set-up, the seat post will move freely and soak up the shocks rather than jarring the rider.

The other ten percent of your "suspension" is tire pressure. The difference between 30psi and 22psi is amazing. The appropriate tire pressure varies according to tire size. The 1938 Chief with 4.50 x 18 tires runs best with 22psi. For 5.00 x 16 tires (usually on spring frame Indians but seldom on rigid frame Indians), use 16psi up front and 18psi in the rear. For 4.00 x 18 tires, use 18psi in front and 20psi for the rear. These tire pressures are for "solo" two-wheeled machines; sidecars and trikes use different pressures. Indian called these the minimum tire pressures, but I recommend not exceeding them unless you're riding double and carrying a lot of baggage.

But, what was wrong with the 1938 Chief fork? First off, the geometry was wrong. Take a look at the accompanying photo, which shows an improperly set-up fork. Notice that the fork rockers are nearly horizontal. The rockers should be angled upward, at an angle of about thirty to forty degrees. Check various photos in this book, and you'll see this.

So, what's the deal? The relationship between the fork rockers, the bellcranks, and the spring leafs, is like the relationship between a crankshaft, a connecting rod, and a piston. In an engine, the piston moves at its greatest speed near the point where the crankshaft and connecting rod are at a ninety-degree angle. In the same way, in a leaf

1920 Model W-20. From 1916 through 1920, Indian sold a single-cylinder commercial model. This is the last of the breed. Hill/Bentley

spring fork, when the rockers are nearly horizontal they are angled at nearly ninety degrees from the bellcranks. This means the bellcranks try to move the spring leafs faster than would be the case if the rockers were angled upward. When angled upward, the rockers are offset from the bellcranks at more than ninety degrees, so that bellcrank movement doesn't produce as much leaf spring movement. Changing the angle of the rockers has the same effect as changing sprocket sizes to alter gear ratios. An improperly setup leaf spring fork is, in a sense, "geared too tall." The improperly setup fork tries to move the leafs too fast, and the leafs resist this with a stiff action. Also, if the rockers are nearly horizontal, you lose the cushioning effect peculiar to a trailing link fork; the wheel can't move slightly rearward when bumped. Shim the spring leafs to get the proper setup.

I suspect there were other problems with this particular 1938 Chief. In all leaf spring forks, when the spring leafs bend, they slide against each other. The leafs must meet minimum sliding resistance in order to give the best possible ride. The 1938 Chief was freshly restored and the black forks glistened with paint that looked like it was still wet. I wondered about the unseen areas between the spring leafs. Was the fork assembled while fresh paint was tacky? At the moment of assembly, were the fork leafs generously coated with oil, or left dry? Certainly, there was no evidence that the leafs had been oiled since restoration.

In thinking about this particular Chief, I recalled a 1940 Chief seen several years ago. The rider had "cheated," that is, used modern technology to improve the ride of the ancient leaf spring fork. He improved the front fork action by having the spring leafs Teflon-coated. Perhaps this is something to consider. Perhaps the softening effect could be achieved by thin Teflon strips between the leafs. In any event, whether by cheating, or by simply running a leaf spring fork with the

1922–24 Standard. For the 1922 season, the name of the cradle spring frame model was changed from "Powerplus" to "Standard." This avoided sending the message that the new 61ci Chief was less powerful than the older model. Also in 1922, the Standard was equipped with new wider front and rear fenders, and with flat sided fender braces. For 1922, a hinge was built into the rear fender to make tire changes easier. The Standard continued basically unchanged in the 1923 and 1924 lineups. This example is a 1924 Standard. Hill/Bentley

original geometry and copious lubrication, you should get a comfortable ride from a leaf spring fork on pavement. Don't be put off by an extremely stiff ride; this problem is fixable.

Indian Four Horror Stories

Since publication of the first edition in 1989, Indian Four horror stories continue to surface. Many of these serious problems are owner-induced. Max Bubeck has started an Indian Four engine restoration service, and he's noted wildly varying piston clearances in the engines sent to him for restoration. The clearance on the upper part of the pistons should be 0.008in and on the lower part 0.006in, just as Indian specified. Examples of misfitting pistons include lower clearances of as little as 0.003in and as great as 0.017in! Additional piston and rings information is provided elsewhere.

Ignition timing is another common problem on Fours. Many owners adjust the ignition timing for a smooth idle when the ignition control is fully advanced. This is incorrect, and any Four set up this way will soon burn its valves because the ignition timing is too retarded. To set the ignition timing properly, comply with the factory specifications. This means that, with the ignition timing fully retarded, the distributor points open when the number one (front) cylinder piston is at top dead center. When the ignition timing is set correctly and the ignition control is fully advanced, the motor will idle with a slightly

1920 Scout, Model G-20. The sensation of the 1920 lineup was the new middle-sized 37ci, 600cc, Scout. Previously, most motorcycles including Indians had a tacked-together look, with lots of little clamps and brackets bringing together the separately built engine, primary drive, and transmission. The Scout had a unit power plant with the transmission bolted to the back of the engine. The two were joined by a helical gear drive running in a cast aluminum oil bath. Scouts weren't available with factory installed electric lights and horn until the 1921 season. The Scout was the basis for the larger Chief which remained in the Indian stable until the end of production in 1953. Hill/Bentley

rough lope. The only way to make a properly adjusted Four idle smoothly is to retard the spark control about 1/8 of a turn.

Occasionally, Fours are observed to have inadequate valve clearances. This information is provided on page 106. If the owner is especially proud of his Four's quietness, he may be guilty of incorrectly adjusting the valves.

Here's Bubeck' theory about why Indian Four engines have so often been butchered by ignorant owners: The typical motorcycling beginner is put off by the construction of a V-twin with its two flywheels and built-up crankpin and drive shafts. The neophyte reasons that V-twin work is over his head and beyond his home workshop. But some beginners look at the Four engine and incorrectly reason that it's merely a smaller version of the family car powerplant. This leads to inadequate or excessive clearances, im-

The 45ci, 750cc, Scout 45 Police Special was launched as a mid-season 1927 model. The new larger motor was still fitted to the old style short Scout frame. Notice the clutch hub legend. 1920 and 1921 Scouts had no legend. 1922, 1923, and early-1924 Scouts and Chiefs had the legend "Hendee Mfg. Co." From mid-1924 forward, Scouts and Chiefs had the Indian Motocycle Co. legend. *Indian Archives/Bob Finn*

proper fitting of piston rings, and, probably, blunders as yet uncataloged.

Fitting Indian Four Pistons, Rings, and Connecting Rods

The correct pistons are of the Robbins design, available from Egge Machine Co., 11707 Slauson Ave., Santa Fe Springs, CA, 90670. These are solid skirt pistons with a "D" cam profile, which causes the skirt to be 0.014 inch narrower across the wrist pin than it is from front to back.

Max Bubeck recommends the following piston and connecting rod fitting steps:

1. Shorten each piston skirt by 3/8 inch.

2. Use only three rings per piston instead of the four per piston used by Indian. On each piston, use two 3/32in compression rings and one 5/32in three-piece oil ring. The oil rings are automotive style, with two thin "rails" and an expander.

3. Modify each expander (grind off as necessary) in order to produce a six- to eight-pound pull test. To test each expander, fit a three-piece oil ring only (no compression rings) to a piston. Using a fish scale, pull the piston through a cylinder. This is an important step because as-delivered expanders are designed for liquid-cooled engines. As-delivered expanders typically produce a twenty-pound pull, which is far too great for air cooled application.

On the 1937 models, the gearshift was moved forward, and the lever was chrome-plated on all but the Junior Scout (previously, Scout Pony). Chiefs and Fours got new quickly detachable and interchangeable wheels. All models had a chrome-plated instrument panel (housing for ammeter and switch). *Hill/Bentley*

4. Bubeck recommends fitting connecting rod inserts instead of using the traditional Babbitt bearings. Some problems have been experienced in recent years with Babbitt bearings, apparently due to lower quality material or to a "lost art" phenomenon. The details of the insert design are too complex to relate here. For sufficient information, contact either of the following:

Max Bubeck
2274 Cardillo
Palm Springs, CA 92262
(619) 323-0304

Larry Struck
21129 Jimmersal
Groveland, CA 95321
(209) 962-5181.

Incidentally, Struck is a master welder and can repair any Four crankcase with no trace left of the repair (that's a fact rather than a slogan).

Attempts To Revive Indian

The history of the Indian trademark is clouded. The company was known as the Hendee Manufacturing Co. until Nov. 1923 when the name was changed to Indian Motocycle Co. In April 1949, Indian Motocycle Co. obtained financial backing from the British firm Brockhouse, and in return set up the Indian Sales Corp. to distribute several brands of English motorcycles alongside Indians. For almost two years, Indian Motocycle Co. acted as sole supplier of Indian motorcycles to the Indian Sales Corp.

Following the failure of the American-made lightweight vertical models, the announcement was made in the Oct. 1951 issue of *Motorcyclist* that all operations had been consolidated under the sales company. Indian Motocycle Co., the announcement continued, had sold all "...inventories, all motorcycle tooling, test equipment, drawings, designs, patterns, and all trademarks relating

1941 Model M1. This model was designed for air-dropping in a crate. The side-valve motor had bore and stroke of 2 1/2x2 3/4in, for a displacement of 13.5ci, 221cc. The primary drive and engine dimensions suggest that the M1 was a fore-runner of the postwar Arrow lightweights. However, the double-tube frame wasn't carried over into the postwar models. Note that the rear brake was heel actuated. *Jimmy Hill*

to production of motorcycles." The announcement concluded, "The Sales Corporation has also acquired exclusive use of the name "Indian" and "motocycle," and the name "motorcycle" when used in connection with the Indian name." In the spring of 1952, the newly consolidated firm was renamed "The Indian Company."

As related in the chapter on imported Indians, Floyd Clymer imported motorcycles and sold them with the traditional Indian script label from 1968 to 1970. Mrs. Meryle Clymer sold the trademark in 1970 to Los Angeles attorney Allan Neuman who founded Indian Motorcycles, Inc., which began importing Italian and Taiwanese mopeds bearing the Indian script logo. Trademark registration then passed to Bankers Trust International, probably as part of credit terms.

When this outfit went bankrupt in 1974, the bankruptcy court auctioned off the name. Outbidding Steve McQueen and Bob Stark was Carmen DeLeone. DeLeone imported Taiwanese mopeds from 1977 through about 1982, using the famous Indian script logo. His firm had the audacity to name a four-stroke version the "Indian Four."

According to recent pretenders to the Indian throne, one or more lapses in the trademark registration occurred between 1952 and 1990. These claims are continuing to enrich lawyers right up to the present.

In 1978, the trademark was registered by the Indian Motorcycle Co., an organization formed by Carmen DeLeone. Registration passed in turn through DeLeone's American Moped Associates to Derbi Motor Corp., importer of the Spanish-built Derbi mopeds. A

When it comes to vibration, you can run but you can't hide. In my nine years of 1947 Chief riding, I found that I could move the vibration around. Standard gearing examples: 55mph was smooth all over; 60mph was smooth on the footboards but rough on the handlebars; 62mph was smooth on the footboards and handlebars but rough around the seat post. After taking up the 62mph habit, I had to change tail pipe clamps about every 3,000mi.

fire at DeLeone's warehouse hastened the end of Derbi sales in 1982 and the trademark was assigned back to DeLeone in 1983.

In 1990, DeLeone sold a half interest in the trademark to Philip S. Zanghi. Zanghi arrived in Springfield, Mass. and claimed he would again build Indians in the area, and that his business would create hundreds of jobs. He placed executive want ads in the Wall Street Journal and promised to resume production by July 4, 1993.

Zanghi then licensed businesses to manufacture Indian clothing and other items, and opened an apparel store in a Springfield mall. He offered to buy a vacant post office for $6.1 million, then pulled out when the property was placed on bid. Later, he claimed to have made a deal to purchase a building in East Windsor, Conn., but that deal also fell through. Then Zanghi bought a small two-story turn of the century brick building in Springfield, upon which he erected a large sign prophesying the return of Indian. The rather decrepit facility was suitable as a small office, warehouse, or workshop, but couldn't loom large in the plans of a company with worldwide aspirations. However, the building did give Zanghi's Indian Motocycle Co. Inc. a Springfield business address.

Zanghi became involved in a dispute

1937 Sport Four. Stuck with an ungainly and unpopular layout, Indian tried to revive sales with twin Zenith carburetors and splashes of chrome. Items getting the chrome treatment were: gearshift lever, saddle connection, ignition cable tube, exhaust pipes, and mufflers. *1937 Indian Dealer's Sales Kit*

with the second aspirant to Indian leadership, Wayne Baughman of Albuquerque, New Mexico. Baughman incorporated his company, Indian Motorcycle Manufacturing, Inc. (IMMI) in May 1990. He began touring motorcycle gatherings, displaying a mockup proposed skirted fender motorcycle minus engine and transmission. Other details on the mockup were sketchy, the whole being more of a styling exercise than an actual prototype.

By 1991, Baughman was working with Diversified Products Group (DPG), a subsidiary of Brunswick Corp., to achieve a powerplant design. Among DPG's accomplishments was the design of the LT5 Corvette engine. DPG collaboration was based on an assumed annual production level of 6,000 60ci, 950cc motorcycles. There were to be two models: the kick start, chain drive Scout with rigid frame; and the electric start, belt drive, Scout 60 with spring frame. Advertised prices, F.O.B. Albuquerque, were $8700 for the Scout and $9600 for the Scout 60.

Baughman disputed DeLeone's and

Zanghi's trademark rights, so more lawyers got in on the action. In the meantime, Zanghi had attempted to hire Indian dealer Bob Stark to build the first 100 of the Zanghi bikes. Stark has said that Zanghi was to provide a facility and pay the operating cost of the whole operation, and Stark was to provide expertise. Zanghi never put up any money, said Stark. Zanghi had some success as a merchandiser, however. He licensed people to put the Indian trademark on jewelry, T-shirts, jackets, trading cards, and even a banjo, said Stark.

In the spring of 1993, Baughman was projecting a Scout 86 (86ci, 1400cc), and he was in association with the Southwest Research Institute (SRI) in San Antonio, Texas. The rigid- and spring-framed Scouts were then projected to sell at $10,850 and $11,750. One thousand Scouts were to be built during 1993. Future plans included a 100ci, 1640cc, four-cylinder model. Other plans discussed publicly included dealer and servicing arrangements. In April, a fire bombing occurred which Baughman described as a $75,000 impact.

In the summer of 1993, at the Sturgis rally, Baughman displayed a mockup with a wooden dummy powerplant, but the rest of the motorcycle appeared complete. A single model was then proposed, the 100ci, 1640cc Century Chief. The 1994 production estimate was 4,000 to 6,000 units. Late in the year, Baughman projected 500 units for 1994, "If we're lucky...." No more mention was made of DPG or SRI. Their new counterparts were Batten Engineering (Romulus, WI) and Western Design Engineering (Jackson, MI). Production for 1996 was projected at 14,040.

Meanwhile, also in the summer of 1993, Zanghi had come to the end of his run, and had went on the run. Bankruptcy court proceedings for his former Indian Motocycle Co., Inc. and Indian Motocycle Apparel and Accessories, Inc., revealed that Zanghi had moved to North Carolina. A request for extradition was denied by the judge. According to court records: Zanghi was under criminal investigation by Springfield's U.S. Postal Inspector's office and U.S. Attorney's office; Zanghi was the subject of separate criminal investigations in California and Georgia; and Zanghi was the subject of at least three criminal investigations as president of the debtors.

In the spring of 1994, "Dealer News" reported that Australian businessman Maurits-Hayim Langridge would pay up to $2.5 million to the Springfield bankruptcy court for the Indian trademark. Langridge would then be able to collect up to $940,000 from debtors of the former Zanghi companies and continue to pursue marketing of the Indian trademark.

In June 1994, in Albuquerque, Baughman displayed two running examples of the Batten-powered Century Chief. The specifications are provided with the accompanying photo. Neither prototype was ridden, but a demonstration engine was run up on a test stand. Baughman claimed that the EPA prohibited operating the prototype bikes.

An *Independent Biker* magazine associate editor, Terry Roorda, reported on his attendance of the Baughman Albuquerque rally.

1938 Four. During 2,000mi of riding the author has experienced one failure. While the Four was cruising at 67mph, the number three rocker arm seized on its shaft (actually a bolt). This caused the rocker arm support tower to bend and crack. In this view, the number three rocker arm has been removed. Moral: air/oil mist rocker lubrication is marginal; inspect periodically and oil as required, especially before long trips.

In his article "A Tale of Two Indians," Roorda said he called the EPA's Motorcycle Certification division in Ann Arbor, Michigan, and talked to the appropriate official, Dave Goode. Goode related that he had never heard of Baughman or Indian Motorcycle Manufacturing, Inc., and that he could find no file on them. Goode added, the EPA does not concern itself with the operation of prototypes and the agency routinely grants exceptions for prototype, racing, and show vehicles. The EPA, he concluded, only gets seriously involved when vehicles are entering the stream of commerce.

In late 1994, Laughing Indian Riders President Don Doody was called by Wayne Baughman. Doody said Baughman told him that Indian Motorcycle Manufacturing, Inc. is still in business. Baughman also said he had shown his two prototype Century Chiefs at the Daytona Octoberfest.

Opposite page
1992 Bubeck Replica. Having just finished the restoration, Max Bubeck turns over the keys to the author. Vark forks yield a wheelbase that splits the difference between a stock Four and a stock Sport Scout. This, and the Vard's weight distribution, produce quick handling. 101 style gearshift and cut-down flywheel produce silent shifting, up and down. Most modifications are bolt-on items, and the bike can be easily returned to near-stock configuration.

Above
1994 Century Chief. Built by Indian Motorcycle Manufacturing Inc., this is one of two prototypes completed as of January 1995. The Batten-designed oil-cooled sixty-degree V-twin has a 100ci, 1640cc, displacement. Dry sump motor features three valves in each combustion chamber, with the valves opened by two camshafts—one for each cylinder. Inlet charges are provided by a fuel injector. The large pod between the cylinders is the oil tank. *Buzz Kanter/Indian Motorcycle Illustrated*

Frame and engine numbers

Diamond frame models

Year	Cylinders	HP	Motor number
1901	1		Prototype
1902	1	1¾	101-243
1903	1	1¾	244-620
1904	1	1¾	621-1167
1905	1	2¼	1168-2349
1906	1	2¼	2350-4048
1907	1	2¼	5000 up
1907	2	4	T100-T499
1908	1	3½	H100-M702
1908	2	5	T500-T1200

Loop frame models

Year	Cylinders	HP	Motor number
1909	1	2¾	1A01-up
1909	1	3½	10A001-up
1909	1	4	40A001-up
1909	2	5	20A001-up
1909	2	7	70A001-up
1910	1	2¾	1B01-up
1910	1	4	40B001-up
1910	2	5	20B001-up
1910	2	7	70B001-up
1911	1	2¾	1C001-up
1911	1	4	40C001-up
1911	2	5	20C001-up
1911	2	7	70C001-up
1912	1	4	40D001-up
1912	2	7	70D001-up
1913	1	4	40E001-up
1913	2	7	70E001-up
1914	1	4	40F001-up
1914	2	7	70F001-up
1915	1	4	40G001-up
1915	2	7	70G001-up
1915	2	7	50G001-up
1916 (K 2 cycle)	1	2½	20H001-up

Loop frame models

Year	Cylinders	HP	Motor number
1916	2	7	70H001-up
1917 (0)	2	2½	30J001-up
1917	1	4	40J001-up
1917	2	7	70J001-up
1917	2	7	RX001-up
1918(0)	2	2½	30K001-up
1918	1	4	40K001-up
1918	2	7	70K001-up
1918	2	?	KRX001-up
1919(0)	2	2½	30M001-up
1919	1	4	40M001-up
1919	2	7	70M001-up
1919 (big valve)	2	7-9	MP001-up

Powerplus, Standard, Scout, Chief, Prince

Year	Cylinders	HP	Motor number
1920	2	Scout	50R00-up
1920	2	Powerplus	70R001-up
1921	2	Scout	50S00-up
1921	2	Powerplus	70S001 & up
1922	2	Scout	50T000-up
1922	2	Chief	80T000-up
1922	2	Standard	70T001-up
1923	2	Scout	50V000-up
1923	2	Chief 61	80V000-up
1923	2	Chief 74	90V000-up
1923	2	Standard	70V001-up
1924	2	Scout	50X000-up
1924	2	Chief 61	80X000-up
1924	2	Chief 74	90X000-up
1924	2	Standard	70X001-up
1925	1	Prince	30Y000-up
1925	2	Scout	50Y000-up
1925	2	Chief 61	80Y000-up
1925	2	Chief 74	90Y000-up
1926	2	Chief 80 prototype	AH1180 only

	21 ci Prince	37 ci Scout	45 ci Scout	61 ci Chief	74 ci Chief	78 ci Four	30.50 ci Pony
1926	AL101-up	AG101-up		AZ101-up	AH101-up		—
1927	BL101-up	BG101-up	BGP101-up	BZ101-up	BH101-up	CA101-209	—
1928	CL101-up	CG101-up, DG101 to DG2637	CGP101-up, DGP101 to DGP4317	CZ101-up	CH101 to CH2224	CA210-up, DA101-DA700	—
1929	—	DG2638-up	DGP4318-up	—	CH2225-up	DA701-up, EA101-EA775	—
1930	—	EG101 to EG924	EGP101 to EGP3080	—	EH101 to EH1535	EA776 to EA1509	—
1931 motor no.	—	EG925-up	EGP3081-up	—	EH1536-up	EA1510-up	—
1931 serial no.	—	SI344-up	G4050	—	H1410-up	A982 up	—
1932 motor no.	—	—	BOC101-up	—	COC101-up	DOC101-up	EOC101-up
1932 serial no.	—	—	203101-up	—	303101-up	403101-up	503101-up

	45 ci Scout	74 ci Chief	78 ci Four	30.50 ci Junior Scout	45 ci Sport Scout	45 ci Motoplane
1933 motor no.	BCC101-up	CCC101-up	DCC101-up	ECC101-up	FCC101-up	FCC101-up
1933 serial no.	233101-up	333101-up	433101-up	533101-up	633101-up	633103-up
1934 motor no.	BCD101-up	CCD101-up	DCD101-up	ECD101-up	FCD101-up	
1934 serial no.	234101-up	334101-up	434101-up	534101-up	634101-up	
1935 motor no.	BCE101-up	CCE101-up	DCE101-up	ECE101-up	FCE101-up	
1935 serial no.	235101-up	335101-up	435101-up	535101-up	635101-up	
1936 motor no.	BCF101-up	CCF101-up	DCF101-up	ECF101-up	FCF101-up	
1936 serial no.	236101-up	336101-up	436101-up	536101-up	636101-up	
1937 motor no.	BCG101-up	CCG101-up	DCG101-up	ECG101-up	FCG101-up	
1937 serial no.	237101-up	337101-up	437101-up	537101-up	637101-up	
1938 motor no.	—	CCH101-up	DCH101-up	ECH101-up	FCH101-up	
1938 serial no.	—	338101-up	438101-up	538101-up	638101-up	
1939 motor no.	—	CCI101-up	DCI101-up	ECI101-up	FCI101-up	
1939 serial no.	—	339101-up	439101-up	539101-up	639101-up	
1940 motor no.	—	CDO101-up	DDO101-up	EDO101-up	FDO101-up	
1940 serial no.	—	340101-up	440101-up	540101-up	640101-up	
1941 motor no.	—	CDA101-up	DDA101-up	EDA101-up	FDA101-up	
1941 serial no.	—	341101-up	441101-up	541101-up	641101-up	
1942 motor no.	—	CDB101-up	DDB101-up	—	FDB101-up	
1942 serial no.	—	342101-up	442101-up	—	642101-up	

	45 ci Scout	74 ci Chief	30.50 ci Lightweight	45 ci Shaft Drive
Military model motor no.	FDO-101-up	CDO-101-up	GDA-101-up	HDA-101-up
Military model serial no.	640-101-up	340-101-up	741-101-up	841-101-up
Canadian military motor no.		CAV-101-up		
Canadian military serial no.		CAV-101-up		

No civilian production in 1943

Motor and serial numbers by year

	45ci Scout	74ci Chief	30.50ci Lightweight	45ci Shaft Drive	
1944 motor no.	—	CDD101-up	—	—	—
1944 serial no.	—	344101-up	—	—	—
1945 motor no.	—	CDE101-up	—	—	—
1945 serial no.	—	345101-up	—	—	—
1946 motor no.	—	CDF101-up	—	—	—
1946 serial no.	—	346101-up	—	—	—

	Engine size	Model	Number
1947 motor no.	74ci	Chief	CDG101-up
1947 serial no.	74ci	Chief	347101-up
1948 motor no.	45ci	Daytona Scout	FDH_____
1948 serial no.	45ci	Daytona Scout	misc. (old stock used)
1948 motor no.	74ci	Chief	CDH101-up
1948 serial no.	74ci	Chief	348101-up
*1949 motor no.	74ci	Chief	CDI1001-up
*1949 serial no.	74ci	Chief	3491001-up
1949 motor no.	26ci	Scout	2491001-up
1949 motor no.	13ci	Arrow	ADI101-up
1949 serial no.	13ci	Arrow	149101-up
1950 motor no.	80ci	Chief	CEJ1001-up
1950 serial no.	80ci	Chief	3501001-up
1950 motor no.	13ci	Arrow	AAEJ-1001-up
1950 serial no.	13ci	Arrow	1150-1001-up
1950 motor no.	26ci	Scout	BBEJ-1001-up
1950 serial no.	26ci	Scout	2250-1001-up
1950 motor no.	30.5ci	Warrior	BEJ101-up
1950 serial no.	30.5ci	Warrior	250-101-up
1950 motor no.	30.5ci	Warrior TT	BEJ-1001T-up
1950 serial no.	30.5ci	Warrior TT	250-1001T-up
1951 motor no.	80ci	Chief	C2001-up
1951 serial no.	80ci	Chief	C2001-up
1951 motor no.	30.5ci	Warrior	B-101-up
1951 serial no.	30.5ci	Warrior	B-101-up
1951 motor no.	30.5ci	Warrior TT	B1001T-up
1951 serial no.	30.5ci	Warrior TT	B1001T-up
1952 motor no.	80ci	Chief	CS6001-up
1952 serial no.	80ci	Chief	CS6001-up
1952 motor no.	30.5ci	Warrior	CS4001-up
1952 serial no.	30.5ci	Warrior	CS4001-up
1952 motor no.	30.5ci	Warrior TT	BB1001T-up
1952 serial no.	30.5ci	WarriorTT	B1001T-up

*Early telescope models were advertised as 1950.
*They were skipping numbers to make it appear that production numbers were higher.

Indian finishes

Crankcases and Transmission Cases
1901-1925   painted to match frame
1926-1928   Optional: unpainted or painted to match frame
1929-1953   unpainted

Cylinders
1901-1932   dull nickel plated
1933-1934   black
1935-1942   nickel
1944   some nickel, some black
1946-1953   black

Exhaust headers
1901-1928   singles and twins, dull nickel plated
1929-1936   twins, dull nickel plated
1937-1941   45 and 47 ci twins, chrome plated; 30.50 ci twin, black
1942-1945   twins, black
1946-1953   chrome plated
1927-1937   Fours, aluminum
1938-1942   Fours, black porcelain

Mufflers
1901-1939   black
1940-1941   45 and 74 ci twins and fours, chrome plated; 30.50 ci twin, black

Plating of bits and pieces
1901-1929   bright or dull nickel
1930-1953   some items chrome plated
1931-1953   some items cadmium plated

Tires
1901-1924   white
1925-1953   black

Wheel rims
1901-1916   painted to match frame
1917-1946   black
1947   black, chrome at extra charge
1948-1953   chrome plated

Spokes
1901-1916   nickel plated
1917-1930   black
1931-1953   cadmium plated

Wheel hubs
1901-1916   nickel plated
1917-1953   black

Handlebars
1901-1921   nickel plated
1922-1946   black
1947   black or chrome plated at extra charge
1948-1953   chrome plated

Indian name on tank
1901-1909   block letters exclusively
1910   predominatly block, some script-lettered machines
1911   predominantly script, some block-lettered machines
1912-1939   script exclusively
1940-1941   block letters in teardrop emblem
1942   block letters in teardrop emblem, some with block letters in Indian head emblem
1944-1946   block letters in Indian head emblem
1947-1950   script
1952-1953   script in wing-shaped decal

Frames, tanks, fenders and chainguards
1901-1934   all in matching colors
1935-1953   see yearly specifications

Yearly specifications

1901-1903 Indian (dark) Royal Blue

1904   standard, Indian Royal Blue; optional, vermillion (later called Indian Red) or black

1905   standard, Indian Royal Blue; optional, vermillion, black or dark green

1906   standard, Indian Royal Blue; optional, vermillion or black

1907   standard, Indian Royal Blue; optional, vermillion or dark green

1908   standard, Indian Royal Blue; optional, vermillion, dark green or French Gray

1909-1910 standard, Indian Royal Blue; optional, vermillion or Indian Green

1911   standard, Indian Royal Blue; optional, vermillion

1912   standard, Indian Red; optional, Indian Royal Blue

1913-1916 Indian Red only

1917-1918 standard, Indian Red; optional, olive drab; striping design of two narrow gold stripes bounding black center of about ⅜ in.; striping around outlines of tanks and fenders; wheel rims, hubs and spokes black

1919   standard, Indian Red; optional, Indian Gray; 1917-1918 striping design

1920-1923 all models: standard, Indian Red; optional, white or dark blue fine double gold stripes around edges of tanks. Fenders striping, Scout only: crowned and ribbed fenders had fine double gold stripes on either side of the rib about one inch out from the rib; chainguard had fine double gold stripes about ¼ inch from the top. Fenders striping, Chief and Powerplus: fenders were not ribbed; double-line gold striping near outside edges of rear fender; front fender had double-line gold striping around edges of crown and a second set of double-line striping highlighting the valance. Black horn, headlamp and taillamp; bright nickel finish for gearshift lever, kick starter lever, compression release handlever on handlebar, luggage rack and front wheel bellcranks

1924-1926 Chief, same as 1920-1923; Scout striping was changed to single-line; 1925-1926 Prince had single-line striping on tank and no striping on fenders

1927-1929 same as 1924-1925 except Scout fenders were changed to unribbed design, with striping around edges of fenders' crowns like Chief

1930   standard, Indian Red; optional at extra cost, special Indian color combinations; optional solid color or paneled tanks

1931   standard, DuPont Duco Lacquer in Indian Red, gold pinstriping; optional lacquer finishes, black with Japanese Red tank panel, Indian Red with cream tank panel, gray with green tank panel, dark blue with cream tank panel. Special colors at extra cost. Four's pinstriping changed to single-line. Some optional two-color finishes on Scout, Chief and Four used double-line gold pinstriping on fenders to bound the contrasting color

1932   Scout Pony, standard black frame and fenders, Chinese Red tank, gold pinstriping; optional other unspecified finishes. Other 1932 Indians: Indian Red, black, Indian Dark (Police) Blue, and five other unspecified options; gold pinstriping. Note: 1932 literature does not specify whether paint was lacquer or enamel

1933   standard finishes in DuPont Dulux enamel, Indian Red, black, dark blue, cream, Chinese Red, light blue, Indian Red with cream tank panel, black with Chinese Red tank panel, dark blue with light blue tank panel, light blue with Chinese Red tank panel, Chinese Red with black tank panel, light blue with dark blue tank panel, gold pinstriping. Optional extra-cost finishes: any colors available in DuPont Dulux, plus optional color arrangements, plus special tank lettering. Gold pinstriping on all models.

1934   standard finishes in DuPont Dulux enamel, Indian Red, black, dark blue, cream, Chinese Red, light blue, Indian Red with black tank, Indian Red with dark blue tank, Indian Red with cream tank, Indian Red with light blue tank, black with Indian Red tank, black with cream tank, black with Chinese Red tank, black with light blue tank, dark blue with Indian Red tank, dark blue with cream tank, dark blue with Chinese Red tank, dark blue with light blue tank, silver with any standard tank, cream with light blue tank, Chinese Red with cream tank, Chinese Red with light blue tank, light blue with Indian Red tank, light blue with Chinese Red tank, gold pinstriping. Optional extra-cost finishes: any colors available in DuPont Dulux, plus optional color arrangements; gold Indian head transfer on Sport Scout tank only

1935   standard one-color finishes: Indian Red, black, dark blue, silver, Chinese Red. Standard two-color finishes, frame and fork predominating color: dark blue and light blue, dark green and light green, Indian Red and Chinese Red, dark brown and cream brown. Standard three-color finishes, black frame and fork with: light blue and yellow, dark blue and silver, dark blue and

cream, Chinese Red and silver. Gold pinstriping on all Indians; gold Indian head transfer on all tanks. Optional tank trim schemes: solid color tank with choices of standard, arrow or V-top pinstriping arrangement; two-color tank with choices of standard, arrow or V-top arrangement

1936   standard, DuPont Dulux Indian Red, gold pinstriping; optional at no extra charge, a variety of other unspecified color combinations; optional at extra charge, any special colors available in DuPont Dulux; tank trim as in 1935

1937   standard: DuPont Dulux Indian Red, gold pinstriping; optional at no extra charge, a new variety of other color combinations (unspecified); optional at extra charge, any special colors available in DuPont Dulux; tank trim as in 1935 and 1936

1938   standard: first named color on frame, forks and sides of tanks and fenders; second named color on top of tanks and fenders; gold pinstriping with one exception—maroon and orange with green pinstriping—Indian Red, black and Chinese Red, Mohawk Green and Seminole Cream, Navajo Blue and Apache Grey. Tank trim choices of V-top or arrow arrangement, one-color or two-color. Junior Scout in Indian Red only

1939   standard: DuPont Dulux enamel, seven unspecified colors or combinations optional including plain and metallic enamels, new optional World's Fair tank panel designs. New Indian head tank transfers with choices of: face and warbonnet in full-color, red face with black and white warbonnet, face and warbonnet in silver, or traditional face and warbonnet in gold. Gold pinstriping. Optional at extra charge: any special colors available in Dulux. Silver Indian head tank transfers. Junior Scout available in Indian Red or Navajo Blue only, with World's Fair paint scheme only

1940-1945   military finishes, non-gloss olive on frame, forks, tanks, fenders, and chainguard, non-gloss black on wheels, no chrome trim

1940   black frame and forks with tanks, fenders, and chainguard in black, Seafoam (medium) Blue, Brilliant Red, Fallon Brown, Kashan Green or Jade Green

1941   black frame and forks with choice of black, Seafoam Blue, or Brilliant Red on tanks, fenders, and chainguard; complete motorcycle in white; black frame and forks with choice of two-color finishes for tanks and fenders, red and white, blue and white, black and white, black and red, and black and blue—the first color on tanks and fender tops, the second color on fender skirts, chainguard and toolbox

1946   standard, black frame and forks, with tanks, fenders and chainguard in Indian Red, black or Police Silver, painted wheel rims; optional, chrome wheel

rims, tan solo seat. Note: publicity photos show light-color wheel rims with dark-color centers, but chrome rims were phased in

1947 1948   Red, black, and Seafoam Blue

1949   optional Brilliant Red, black, Seafoam Blue, Sunshine Yellow, and turquoise on Arrow and Scout; Arrow wheel rims; standard cadmium plated, optional extra charge chrome plated; Scout rims chrome plated

1950-1951   Arrow, Scout, Warrior, and Chief same colors as 1948-1949 with added option of tangerine on Chiefs; frame, , oil tank, forks and fender braces of Arrow and Scout painted to match fenders and gas tank; frame, oil tank, forks and fenderbraces of Chief, Warrior and Warrior TT in black; Warrior TT, Indian Scarlet only, cadmium plated wheel rims; Chief only, optional tan solo seat without fringes or black chummy seat

1952-1953   same colors as 1950-1951, black upper forks legs on verticals, chrome upper fork legs on Chief, black lower fork legs on all models, optional tan solo seat on Chief without fringes or tan bench-style two-passenger seat

Clubs, dealers, commercial publications

Clubs

Clubs are an excellent source of information. You'll find plenty of dealer and individual advertising to solve any restoration and parts problems you may encounter. To get you started, here's some club information.

The All-American Indian Motorcycle Club, Inc.
Earnie Hartman Jr.
25801 Clark Rd.
Wellington, OH 44090
Established in 1965; publishes a quarterly newsletter. Annual dues are $10.

The Antique Motorcycle Club of America (AMC)
Dick Winger, membership chairman
Box 333
Sweetser, IN 46987
Established in 1954; over 6,000 members; provides contacts for any antique motorcycle need; especially valuable to collectors of older and rarer Indians for which Indian dealer support is not available; eight or nine nationally sanctioned antique motorcycle shows per year, coast to coast; one nationally sanctioned tour per year; many local chapter events. Publishes a quarterly magazine, "The Antique Motorcycle," typically 48 black and white pages and color covers. Annual dues are: U.S.A., $20; Canada, $18; Other Foreign $40; Spouses, $5.

Indian Motorcycle Club of Australia
Jim Parker, President
537 Burke Rd., Hawthorne East 3123
Victoria, Australia
Publishes a newsletter.

The Indian Motorcycle Club of America
Box 1743
Perris, CA 92370
Established in 1972 by Bob and Shorty Stark as an adjunct to their motorcycle business; publishes a monthly newsletter and a semi-annual booklet; many maintenance tips are offered; club discounts for purchases from the motorcycle shop. Annual dues are $25.

The Indian Four Cylinder Club
Richard Davies
Rt. 2, Box 227
Rosedale, IN 47874
Established in 1966; publishes a quarterly newsletter; annual meet in Midwest. Annual dues are $15.

Vintage Motorcycle Club of Australia
The Secretary
167 Rosedale Road
St. Ives, 2075
Publishes newsletter.

Vintage Motorcycle Club of Victoria
The Secretary
167 Rosedale Road
St. Ives 2075
Publishes a newsletter.

The 101 Association Inc.
679 Riverside Ave.
Torrington, CT 06790
Established in 1984; publishes a quarterly booklet with 101 Scout information not available elsewhere; annual meeting in conjunction with an AMC nationally sanctioned event. Annual dues are $15 for US, $22.50 for foreign members.

Laughing Indian Riders
Don Doody
1114 237A St.
RR 9 Langley, BC V3A 6H5 Canada
Established in 1984; publishes a quarterly newsletter emphasizing Indian history; much information on Indian personalities and current events in antique motorcycling; tech tips. Annual dues are $15.00.

Military Vehicle Collectors Club
Box 33697AM
Thornton, CO 80233
Publishes technical magazine quarterly; publishes advertising journal six times per year. Annual dues are $20 for US, $35 for foreign members.

Dealers

With apologies for anyone whom I may have overlooked, the following were the Indian businesses at the time of publication.

American Indian Motorcycle Co.
486 Rich Gulch Rd.
Mokelumne Hill, CA 95245
Parts for Chiefs, Sport Scouts and other models; catalog published.

American Indian Specialists
1101H East Ash Ave.
Fullerton, CA 92631

(714) 447-4636
Fax (714) 447-8346
   Restoration, maintenance, and performance up-
grades for Indians.

Sam Avellino
240 Harris St
Revere, MA 02151
   Royal Enfield and Enfield Indian parts.

Robert D. Beard
1241 Pinehurst Dr.
Fort Wayne, IN 46815
   Headlamps for Indians and other marques.

Beard Machine, Inc.
18 Highland Ave.
Long Valley, NJ 07853
(908) 277-0217
   New old-style bolts, nuts and washers used
from 1920s to 1950s.

Tom Bethel
(518) 459-2535
   Speedometer repair and restoration, Stewart-
Warner and Corbin.

Bob's Indian Sales
RD#3 Box 3449
580 Old York Rd.
(717) 938-2556
Uniquely knowlegable in restoration details for
30s and 40s models
Etters, PA 17319
   Parts and service.

Bollenbach Engineering
296 Williams Place
East Dundee, IL 60118-2319
(708) 428-2800
Fax (708) 428-0774
   Complete restorations, engine and transmission
rebuilding, service.

Brownie's Indian Sales & Service
280 Broadway
Rensselaer, NY 12144

Max Bubeck
The Indian 4 Experience
2274 Cardillo Ave.
Palm Springs, CA 92262
(619) 323-0304
   Copper head gaskets for 1938-1942 Fours, laser
cut, dealer discounts. Indian Four engine rebuilding, including modifications for modern road riding. Indian Four restoration video available.

Woody Carson
518 Edwards St.
Ft. Collins, CO 80524
(970) 416-0060
   Indian carburetor covers 1928-1934, cast brass
carburetor covers for 101 Scout (not plated); cast
brass Corbin speedometer head brackets #S195 (not
plated).

John and Nancy Casteras
14 Water St.
Colonia, NJ 07067-2818
(908) 388-9236
Fax (908) 388-9236 (same number as regular phone)
   Pre-1930s reproduction parts, many hard-to-get
items such as "S" shaped brake lever, front and rear
101 Scout fenders, etc.

Classics East
Box 1406
Statesville, NC

Bill Clymer
3707 Otis Rd. S.E.
Cedar Rapids, IA 52401
   Early gas caps with primer, early ignition switch
levers.

Coker Tire
1317 Chestnut St.
Box 72554
Chattanooga, TN 37407
(800) 251-6336
   Tires for early American makes.

Coles Ignition & Mfg.
52 Legionaire Dr.
Rochester, NY 14617
   Wiring harnesses.

Tony Conley
56 Main St.
Dresden, NY 14441
   Heli-arc welding to repair motorcycle crankcases.

Dave's Motorcycle Parts
23106 Forest Ln.
Taylor, MI 48180

Dick and Lavera Davies
RR 2, Box 227
Rosedale, IN 47874-9370
(812) 877-9331
   Indian Four parts, hard-to-get items.